IDENTITY THIEVES

HEITH COPES & LYNNE M. VIERAITIS

IDENTITY THIEVES
MOTIVES AND METHODS

NORTHEASTERN UNIVERSITY PRESS | BOSTON

Northeastern University Press
An imprint of University Press of New England
www.upne.com
© 2012 Northeastern University
All rights reserved
Manufactured in the United States of America
Composed in Warnock Pro type from Adobe

University Press of New England is a member of the Green Press Initiative.
The paper used in this book meets their minimum requirement for recycled paper.

For permission to reproduce any of the material in this book, contact Permissions,
University Press of New England, One Court Street, Suite 250, Lebanon NH 03766;
or visit www.upne.com

Library of Congress Cataloging-in-Publication Data
     Copes, Heith.
     Identity thieves: motives and methods / Heith Copes & Lynne M. Vieraitis.
          p. cm.
     Includes bibliographical references.
     ISBN 978-1-55553-786-9 (cloth: alk. paper)—ISBN 978-1-55553-767-8
(pbk.: alk. paper)—ISBN 978-1-55553-768-5 (ebook)
     1. Identity theft—United States. 2. Fraud—United States. I. Vieraitis, Lynne M.
II. Title.
     HV6679.C67 2012
     364.16'330973—dc23
     2011042353

5 4 3 2 1

CONTENTS

FOREWORD

Examined over the span of centuries, images of crime—and of the faces of those who commit crimes—create a shifting mosaic. Crimes once commonplace disappear or decline in significance, while newer ones appear and take on greater importance in the public mind. Stalking, environmental degradation, and Internet child pornography were not part of crime in most Western nations until late in the twentieth century. When new crimes are designated and gain attention, control experts typically promote self-interested and almost certainly exaggerated notions about the threat they pose. Likewise, the challenge of responding to the new criminals is sketched as an unusually difficult one that demands increased attention and resources. Because of these historical dynamics, shining an empirical light on emergent forms of crime becomes an important job. Doing so can challenge or correct weakly substantiated claims and help arbitrate disputes on the basis of evidence. This excellent book by Heith Copes and Lynne Vieraitis performs this valuable task for identity theft and exploitation, and for claims about the nature of those who commit these crimes.

Identity theft appears to be as old as organized commerce, but the means by which it is accomplished—and its consequences— changed dramatically in the years just prior to the onset of the twenty-first century. As its prevalence increased, so did the level of fear and anxiety reported by ordinary citizens. The timing of this book's appearance could scarcely be better. The portrait it presents of those who steal and exploit others' identities may surprise readers and correct misinformation. Whether or not it will allay anxiety and fear is another matter.

Identity Thieves gives us the first close-up look at men and women convicted and sentenced for identity theft that is based on a sample large enough to warrant generalization. Copes and Vieraitis find that not all identity theft is cut from the same cloth; it can be committed by offenders with lengthy criminal records or by criminal neophytes. The techniques for successfully committing it are neither so complex nor arcane as to defy independent invention and use. Identity theft is committed by solitary individuals as well as by groups of criminals in ad hoc organizations with specialized roles. Some identity thieves appear but one or two short steps removed from the underclass and a *lumpenproletariat* of criminal acquisition, but others have outwardly respectable middle-class backgrounds and lives. Similarly, a continual quest for monies to support consumption of illicit drugs drives some, but not all, identity thieves.

This diversity in identity theft is important for what it suggests about larger problems of white-collar crime, efforts to explain it and to fashion control responses, and divergent opinions as to what these responses should be. For many investigators, it is the materially and morally privileged worlds of *offenders* that distinguishes and justifies the theoretical designation and examination of white-collar crime; for others, however, it is the qualities of criminal *offenses*, without regard to the social characteristics of its perpetrators.

Most street criminals would say that white-collar criminals generally do not "rip it off," but "talk it off" instead. It is this operating style that makes them white-collar criminals, and that style fairly describes a large part of the conduct of identity thieves. Still, they and their crimes differ glaringly from the demographics, lives, and crimes of *upperworld* white-collar criminals. International investment bankers, national political leaders, and similarly situated criminals have little in common with identity thieves, bankruptcy fraudsters, criminal telemarketers, mortgage origination fraudsters, insurance fraudsters, and other *ordinary* white-collar offenders. In their backgrounds, lives, and perspectives the two groups are strikingly different.

As ordinary white-collar criminals, the ways in which identity thieves differ among themselves are notably similar to what has been found in studies of comparable offender samples. A substantial proportion of ordinary white-collar criminals have official histories of street-crime participation, for example, and yet offenses that differ in no important way also are committed by offenders whose lives and crimes amply justify what they have been called: crimes of the middle-class.

There are clear theoretical pointers and lessons in this book. One obvious message involves the consequences of the veritable explosion of opportunities for ordinary white-collar crime in recent decades. The positive relationship between the supply of white-collar criminal opportunities and the variation in white-collar crime can be interpreted in a straightforward fashion using the logic of theories of crime-as-choice. Many readers will probably be surprised by what Copes and Vieraitis have to say about decision-making by identity thieves. The absence of the causal variables which figure prominently in explanations of upperworld white-collar crime also is noteworthy. Wealth, power, and the use of legitimate organizations in the commission of crimes seem to play no part in the narratives of identity thieves. The contrast with upperworld crime is stark.

Because their work is based on interviews with incarcerated offenders, some readers may wonder how accurately this portrait of identity thieves reflects their larger population. It is an understandable concern, though perhaps one that cannot be resolved with confidence today; at this point, the corpus of research on diverse samples of identity thieves is insufficiently large. It would be well if evidence gathering allows a credible resolution to this question, and if diverse assumptions about offender variation follow a pattern different from that pursued by critics of comparable research on imprisoned street criminals. Bourgeois criminologists may be unusually prone to imagining a population of unarrested, unconvicted, or unimprisoned criminals that differs conspicuously from the demographic characteristics, lifestyles, and decision-making of prisoners convicted of similar crimes. These fanciful if not romanticized notions can be sustained only by ignoring research. Decades of study have shown that, for street criminals, the evidence is unambiguous, unassailable, and undisputed by ethnographers: there are no significant points of disagreement between ethnographies of offenders unknown to authorities and ethnographies of those who are in the clutches of the criminal justice system. The same may prove to be true of a high proportion of offenders who work the potentially high-yielding ore of ordinary white-collar crime.

Neal Shover
Professor Emeritus
University of Tennessee

ACKNOWLEDGMENTS

This book is the culmination of our concerted effort to interview identity thieves and organize their accounts. The idea of the project came about when the two of us, who had worked across the hall from each other for several years, concluded that collaboration would be fruitful and rewarding. After brainstorming on potential projects, we serendipitously found an article on identity theft and realized this was the direction to move in. We decided to submit a grant proposal to the National Institute of Justice (NIJ). Because of the low number of qualitative projects funded by NIJ, neither of us expected a positive decision, but we caught lightning in a bottle and were awarded the grant. The grant gave us the opportunity (or forced us, depending on one's point of view) to travel across the country. While it was a great deal of work, we also learned a great deal.

While conducting this research on identity thieves, our goals were to explore how their lifestyles and associations with others contribute to criminal decision-making, including how they account for their crimes, how they evaluate and manage the risks of stealing identities, and how they organize to carry out the act. In providing answers to these questions, we drew primarily upon rational-choice theory to interpret what the offenders said and to provide a comprehensive framework for understanding how identity thieves made sense of and carried out their acts. As a result, the book is structured in a manner comparable with other work using rational-choice theory. We hope to present the crime in a way that is true to the lived experiences of the culprits, a hallmark of sound ethnographic research.

None of this would have been possible without the help and support of numerous people. We begin with thanks to the National Institute of Justice, Office of Justice Programs, U.S. Department of

Justice, who graciously funded this research endeavor (Grant No. 2005-IJ-CX-0012). Without their support we certainly would not have been able to start, much less finish, this undertaking. During the project, which took a little longer than expected, we were able to work with two excellent grant managers: Maggie Heisler and Christine Crossland. We thank them for their hard work, insights, and patience. The points of view or opinions expressed in this work are those of the authors and do not necessarily represent the official position or policies of the U.S. Department of Justice.

Our ability to carry out the research was facilitated by employees at the Federal Bureau of Prisons. Victoria Joseph and Jody Klein-Saffran made our travel and our lives much easier. They were a treat to work with and represented their organization well. We also thank the various wardens and other staff members at the fourteen institutions we visited. These people are the ones who we inconvenienced the most and we are greatly appreciative of their willingness to adjust their schedules and help us.

Our research assistants—Crystal Null, Martha Mears, Rachael Donovan, and Anastasia Brown—were asked to do much of the monotonous work. They helped us search newspapers, copy articles, transcribe interviews, and format references. In short, they helped with the more tedious tasks and we appreciate their efforts tremendously.

We are grateful to the sixty-five individuals who trusted us enough to tell their stories, even though they did not know us. Despite our inability to offer them any tangible benefits, they answered our calls and provided details about their lives and crimes, some of which were painful to relive. Indeed, without them this project and the resulting products (including this book) could not have been possible. We wish them well in their reformations.

We also thank Claire Renzetti, who brought our research to the attention of Phyllis Deutsch, editor-in-chief of University Press of New England. Although we had talked about writing a book about the identity thieves we interviewed, it was their interest in our work that kindled the spark to actually write it. We are further indebted to Phyllis for pushing us to improve upon earlier versions of our manuscript.

In preparing our manuscript we sought help and suggestions from several people. Robert Morris, Andy Hochstetler, Bruce Jacobs, and John Sloan were wonderful in this regard. They read early versions of the chapters and offered comments and criticisms that improved the book immensely. While we would like to blame them for any theoretical missteps in the manuscript, this would be untrue. In fact, they helped keep us on the right path throughout. Any strayings from this are our mistakes alone.

While writing the book we adapted portions of our previously published work, "Understanding Identity Theft: Offenders' Accounts of Their Lives and Crimes," *Criminal Justice Review* 34 (2009): 329–349, and "Bounded Rationality of Identity Thieves: Using Offender-Based Research to Inform Policy," *Criminology and Public Policy* 8 (2009): 237–262. We thank Sage and the American Society of Criminology for their permission to reprint.

Finally we thank our families for carrying the burdens of daily life while we trekked around the country. Our spouses—Buffy Copes and Tom Kovandzic—were incredibly understanding during the many months of travel. Despite the inconveniences of air travel, the trips were fun, but it was always nice coming home to them. Thank you also to Sheila and Ron Vieraitis, who made these trips possible by providing child care; to Katie, who did her best to make things easier when mommy was on a "work trip"; and to Courtney, who we hope is not adversely affected by her many visits to prison. We dedicate this book to our families.

IDENTITY THIEVES

INTRODUCTION

The 2002 movie *Catch Me If You Can* portrayed the life and crimes of Frank Abagnale, perhaps one of the most famous fraudsters in American history. He gained notoriety for the young age (sixteen) at which he began his crimes, and for the daring and creative methods he used to con people into thinking he was a Pan Am airline pilot, a pediatrician in Atlanta, and an attorney in the Louisiana attorney general's office, to name a few of his impersonations. Although the bulk of his crimes involved forgery, without the use of other people's identities, he did engage in identity theft earlier in his criminal career. After all, he couldn't cash a check without a bank account, and opening an account required some form of identification. To commit his crimes, Abagnale needed more than one account and more than one identity. During five years on the run, Abagnale defrauded banks of an estimated $2.5 million.

This level of success required a great deal of skill, effort, and access to expensive, hard-to-find equipment. Occurring before the large-scale computerization of personal records and the birth of the Internet, Abagnale's task required physical trips to departments of vital records for copies of death certificates. Using the identities of deceased infants who shared the year of his birth (1948), Abagnale secured a driver's license in every state. Creating fraudulent checks was even more difficult. Readers may recall a scene in *Catch Me If You Can* in which Abagnale (played by Leonardo DiCaprio) climbs the scaffolding surrounding an enormous printer, to load the paper necessary to produce company payroll checks. The printer, purchased at a cost of $1 million, was ninety feet long and eighteen feet high.[1]

Moviegoers were likely in awe of Abagnale's enterprising methods and the sheer audacity with which he conned people. These

1

fascinating aspects of his story made it worthy of a Hollywood movie but, precisely because they were so extraordinary, most viewers sensed that few people could have been as successful as Abagnale at such frauds. Similarly, the daring schemes and high costs certainly would have discouraged Abagnale's contemporaries from considering such fraud as a viable way to obtain money. In short, most people simply couldn't have done what he did.

Flash forward to the first decade of the twenty-first century and the opportunity for fraud is quite different. Identity thieves now can be successful even if they don't possess the cunning and charisma of Frank Abagnale. Whereas he had to charm information from those in charge of data (what hackers call social engineering), contemporary identity thieves can simply send phishing e-mails, locate discarded information, or hire people to log on to computers and access identifying information. Advancements in computer technology and networking have provided offenders with new tools and emerging opportunities to steal or exploit information for profit. Consider how technology has changed the ways people communicate and conduct everyday transactions. From the comfort of your own home, you can use a relatively inexpensive computer to register for classes at the local college, order phone service, "chat" with a friend living across the globe through instant messaging, and purchase merchandise not available in your home town. Without a doubt, such reliance on technology has created new opportunities for those inclined toward fraud.

Although the use of technology to communicate and conduct everyday business is convenient, it also has a downside. By participating in these electronic transactions, you might be making your personal information—including name, address, social security number, credit card numbers, or passwords—vulnerable to theft. To steal such information, an identity thief merely has to find a company employee willing to retrieve it, or hire the services of a computer hacker who can access data from another location. While technology has made it easier to quickly retrieve large amounts of information, it also has made it easier to illegally turn that information into profit. Remote transactions make it simpler for thieves to pose as others. After opening bank or credit card accounts from the safety of a computer, thieves can then shop for merchandise at brick-and-mortar stores or simply place orders online and never have to come in contact with another person.

Advances in digital technology also have made it simpler and cheaper to forge paper documents. If Abagnale was committing his crimes now, he would likely be sitting at home, using software to create company checks on his laptop computer and printing them with a laser printer—equipment which can be purchased at any office supply store. His access to victims' personally identifying information would likely be easier to come by as well since he wouldn't have to physically visit a department of vital records. As a seasoned con man, he could simply talk people out of their information while posing as any of a number of professionals who routinely require clients to identify themselves. Or, like many identity thieves today, he could just pay someone at a business or agency whose work requires the handling and storage of personal data to steal the information and bring it to him.[2]

It is true that hackers and phishers are responsible for a sizable amount of fraud, including identity theft; however, research suggests that only 10 percent of identity theft cases originate online.[3] Thieves who use less sophisticated measures, like dumpster diving and mailbox raiding, may be responsible for greater losses than cybercriminals.[4] The ease with which those with an eye toward fraud can find and exploit security lapses in the banking and credit industries, as well as society's increasing reliance on a cashless economy, have likely contributed to the rapid increase in identity theft since the turn of the twenty-first century. And the ubiquity of identity thieves in the news suggests that movie producers have many potential subjects for another biopic like Frank Abagnale's. Current estimates place the number of identity theft victims at between 8 and 12 million per year.[5] If these estimates are accurate, the number of people who have engaged in identity theft is quite large indeed.

Hardly a day goes by that we do not hear about a new scam to steal personal information, the dangers of conducting routine transactions, or the latest products and services designed to protect us from those who wish to profit from our names. Without a doubt, media coverage of identity theft also has risen dramatically since the turn of the new century. Although much of this attention is directed toward educating consumers and marketing identity theft protection products, the media regularly present identity theft as an unstoppable and ever-increasing problem.[6] Whereas the media seemed fascinated with Abagnale because of his extraordinary qualities, they seem fascinated with the rising generation of identity thieves because of their ubiquity.

Current estimates about the prevalence and extent of identity theft are quite staggering; unfortunately, as with many frauds, it is difficult to ascertain a true picture of the pervasiveness and costs of identity theft based on the available data. As mentioned above, the estimated number of victims is between 8 and 12 million annually; the estimated cost ranges from $16 billion to $50 billion per year. One reason for the differences in estimates is that not all agencies define identity theft in the same way. Such ambiguity has led to much confusion on exactly what crimes should be considered identity theft. In 1998, the U.S. Congress passed the Identity Theft Assumption and Deterrence Act (ITADA) making identity theft a federal offense and charging the Federal Trade Commission with collecting complaints from consumers. As part of the ITADA, codes were enacted to prohibit the theft and unlawful use of personally identifying information.[7] Prior to the passage of ITADA, federal law only prohibited the fraudulent creation, use, or transfer of identification documents,[8] and not the theft or criminal use of the underlying personal information.[9] According to the federal identity theft statute, it is unlawful if a person "knowingly transfers, possesses or uses, without lawful authority, a means of identification of another person with the intent to commit, or to aid or abet, or in connection with, any unlawful activity that constitutes a violation of Federal law, or that constitutes a felony under any applicable State or local law." The term "means of identification" contained in the law is defined as "any name or number that may be used, alone or in conjunction with any other information, to identify a specific individual, including any (a) name, social security number, date of birth, official state or government issued driver's license or identification number, alien registration number, government passport number, employer or taxpayer identification number; (b) unique biometric data, such as fingerprint, voice print, retina or iris image, or other unique physical representation; or (c) unique electronic identification number, address or routing code; or telecommunication identifying information or an access device."[10] Although the 1998 federal statute supplied the first legal definition of identity theft, a report by the Bureau of Justice Statistics (the agency responsible for collecting data for the National Crime Victimization Survey), stated that "there is no one universally accepted definition of identity theft as the term describes a variety of illegal acts involving theft or misuse of personal information."[11]

While no definitive description of the crime exists, a common theme of most definitions is the idea that identity theft is "the misuse of another individual's personal information to commit fraud."[12] But what does "personal information" mean? If an offender steals a credit card, makes a purchase, and then disposes of the card, has the victim's identity been stolen? Does *any* misuse of a financial account identifier or personally identifying data constitute identity theft?

Consider the following two scenarios, which are based on the interviews we conducted. In the first scenario, Jake uses his computer at work to access people's names, birthdates, and social security numbers, then uses this data to open fraudulent credit card accounts and make purchases at various online retailers.[13] Here the offender illegally accesses personally identifying information (the names, birthdates, and social security numbers of persons in his employer's database) and uses that information to make unlawful purchases. This case is clearly one of identity theft.

In contrast, consider this scenario: Chandra steals lists of customer credit-card numbers from the gas station where she works. She then sells the numbers (financial account identifiers) to two friends, who in turn use the numbers to purchase merchandise at online stores. Here, Chandra only steals the financial account identifiers. She obtains no other personally identifying information, such as names, birthdates, addresses, or social security numbers. Further, she does not pose as the legitimate owners of the credit cards. Instead, her two friends make the fraudulent purchases. Should Chandra's actions be considered identity theft? As should be evident, some crimes are difficult to classify.

The question becomes, should the label "identity theft" be applied only to situations in which personally identifying information is stolen? Or can the actions of the offenders described in the two scenarios be considered identity theft? Some argue that we should use different labels to describe the two parts of the crime: "identity theft" and "identity fraud." The acquisition of personally identifying information is identity theft, while the use of such information for the purposes of opening accounts or writing checks is identity fraud.[14] The answers to these questions can have dramatic impacts on estimates of the prevalence and costs of the crime and on portraits of victims and offenders. For example, the inclusion of credit card fraud using existing accounts dramatically influences the profile of identity theft victims. Specifically including these types of frauds, which are more prevalent than other types of identity theft, creates the impression that all citizens have an equal chance of becoming victims, when this is not the case. The inclusion of existing credit card fraud also may hide the fact that low-income people are at a higher risk of being victimized by the more financially harmful (at least for individuals) types of identity theft.[15] It is clear that having a consistent definition, and agreeing on which types of crimes fall under that definition, are important for understanding this crime and developing effective control policies.

Despite the rise in attention to identity theft, a great deal about this crime remains unknown. Perhaps the largest gap in knowledge concerns the most likely perpetrators. Most of what we know about identity thieves comes from closed case reports, either from the U.S. Secret Service or local police departments.[16] Government and consumer agencies have developed campaigns to educate the public on the types of information identity thieves seek out, what thieves do with such information, and the steps consumers can take to protect themselves from becoming victims. However, much of this information is based on victim reports or law enforcement agents' assumptions about who steals identities and how they do it. Some of it has even been produced by for-profit companies, at least a few of which rely on fear to sell unneeded or incomplete protection.[17]

Until now, there has yet to be a systematic study that seeks the perspective of those who arguably know the most about the crime—the thieves themselves.[18] We can learn a great deal from talking to both victims and law enforcement officers about identity theft; however, the danger of privileging victim and law enforcement perspectives about any crime is that it may lead to distorted and incomplete understandings about causes and consequences, thus hindering the development of solutions. For example, many adherents of the "broken windows perspective" suggest that unkempt lawns, unattended buildings, and unaddressed graffiti are clear signs to criminals and others that residents have given up on their communities.[19] This outsider perspective—typically offered by academics or public officials—is widely accepted as the "truth" about residents' attitudes. However, the inhabitants of these neighborhoods offer a different interpretation of physical decay: it is evidence that city leaders have abandoned *them.* Moreover, criminals don't always select targets based on the physical condition of neighborhood structures, as the theory suggests.[20] By asking residents and offenders to describe their perceptions of crime, we can gain a deeper understanding of the problem and its causes.

We think that it is vitally important to obtain the identity thief's perspective if we are to truly understand, respond to, and prevent this pervasive crime. Others agree with this general perspective. In fact, some have suggested that "[t]here can be no more critical element in understanding and ultimately preventing crime than understanding the criminal's perceptions, opportunities and risks associated with [the type of crime in question]."[21]

This book explores the crime of identity theft through the narratives of offenders. We seek to obtain the answers to questions such as, Who engages in identity theft? Why do they choose to commit identity theft rather than other forms of crime? How do they organize themselves to commit their crimes? How do they gain access to someone's personal identifying information? What do they do with the information once it is in their possession? What do they perceive to be the rewards of their behaviors? What risks do they associate with their crimes and how do they overcome their aversion to these risks? And, finally, how do they make sense of their illicit actions? By looking at the answers to these questions, we will better understand the motives for choosing identity theft, the methods used to commit it, and the meaning all of this has for developing informed theory and policy.

We collected narratives by traveling across the country, interviewing identity thieves incarcerated in federal prisons. With the help of the Federal Bureau of Prisons, we were able to interview fifty-nine individuals convicted of identity theft. We conducted the interviews between February 2006 and March 2007. These interviews, which lasted from forty-five minutes to two hours, were semi-structured and designed to explore offenders' life circumstances at the time of their crimes, their reasons for becoming involved in and continuing with identity theft, and the techniques they used to secure information and convert it into cash or goods. (A more detailed description of our methods appears in the appendix.) Our goal was to have the participants tell their own stories.

To locate these individuals, we examined newspapers and legal documents from across the nation and searched press releases from each U.S. attorney's Web site. We then used the Federal Bureau of Prisons' Inmate Locator to determine if the people whose names we had collected resided in the federal prison system.[22] Our search yielded the names of 297 identity thieves who were being housed in federal prisons. It was from this list that we drew our sample. In total we visited fourteen federal correctional facilities across the United States.

When analyzing the narratives of offenders, it is often difficult to know which storylines are important. Researchers often look to theory for insight. Having a theoretical framework in mind not only helps structure the interview questions, but also helps make sense of the stories embedded in voluminous pages of transcripts. We were interested primarily in the ways that identity thieves made the decision to engage in their crimes and in the ways that they enacted these crimes. Because of this focus, our interpretation of their accounts is consistent with recent developments in criminal decision-making research. The bulk of recent research on this topic is grounded in "rational choice theory" and assumes that offenders evaluate the potential penalties of crime against its anticipated rewards before choosing a course of action. While we incorporated a variety of theoretical approaches both while constructing interview questions and in the subsequent analyses (for example, differential association and the sociology of accounts), the majority of the book is informed by recent insights from rational choice theory.

RATIONAL CHOICE THEORY

Rational choice theorists argue that individuals pursue goals that reflect their self-interests and purposively choose to commit crime if the expected benefits of criminal behavior exceed the benefits of engaging in legitimate behavior. Conversely, the decision to forgo criminal behavior is based on the individual's perception that the benefits are too low or the risk of detection and subsequent costs are too high. In other words, individuals are thought to explore all of their options and choose the course of action that provides them with the highest expected return. It is believed that after a brief mental calculation, decisions to engage in criminal behavior are based largely on which behavior among alternatives is likely to result in the greatest net gain. From this standpoint, criminality is not a disposition but rather a choice. Economists, cognitive psychologists, and many others in criminology have offered models of criminal decision-making grounded in these assumptions.[23]

Early rational choice theorists borrowed from economic theories and proposed models of criminal decision-making that could be expressed mathematically. These theories depicted offenders as "pure" rational calculators; that is, as actors who are thought to optimize their behaviors by rationally analyzing all relevant information that is available to them (for example, probability of arrest, severity of sanctions, amount of effort involved) and then choosing behaviors that yield the highest expected benefits for the lowest costs. Such theorists imagine offenders as self-maximizing decision makers who carefully calculate costs and benefits before acting.

This narrow interpretation of humans as purely rational calculators has been criticized from several academic perspectives.[24] Perhaps the most telling criticism observes that this self-maximizing model of criminal behavior seems to be at odds with the "opportunistic, ill-considered, and even reckless nature of much crime."[25] To better understand the decision-making process of offenders, investigators began examining the ways in which offenders evaluate their options and choose crime within a sociocultural context. This line of research eschewed the quantitative methods that characterized earlier rational choice studies for qualitative ones, thereby producing data on criminal decision-making from the perspective of the offender. These studies examined the components of criminal decisions, including the decision to commit crime instead of pursuing legitimate alternatives, the process of selecting targets, and the perceptions of the various rewards and costs of crime.

This growing empirical emphasis on understanding the decision-making process of offenders led to more cautious and subjective theoretical understandings of criminal choice, or what has been termed "limited" or "bounded" rationality.[26] Whereas economists presume that aspects of the criminal calculus—probability of arrest, sanction severity, and potential rewards—are based on accurate and objective perceptions, those espousing bounded models argue that such information is subjectively acquired, stored, and recalled. This subjectivity not only creates inadequate information and cognitive processing, but also further confounds rational decision-making when cognitive heuristics—mental shortcuts humans rely on to process information but which are subject to systematic error—are used during probability assessment. Thus, bounded rationality implies that both the amount and the accuracy of our information are constrained by our cognitive capacities to acquire and process that information and, as a result, human behavior is not rational in the strict sense of expected utility maximization.[27]

Bounded models of criminal decision-making take into account the social, physical, and situational contexts in which criminal decisions are made, as well as offenders' perceptions of the world around them. This implies that offenders subjectively assess costs and benefits and that their assessments are fluid. Under the right circumstances, risks that once deterred might become manageable while rewards that were previously overlooked might turn into powerful lures. The reverse is also possible: rewards can lose their luster while risks can grow more threatening, leading the offender to forego crime. Thus, to better understand the decision-making process of offenders, it is necessary to situate their decisions within the principal lifestyle that frames their choices.[28] Interviews with persistent street offenders suggest that many of them emphasize the enjoyment of good times at the expense of almost everything else. They live in a social world that emphasizes partying and fast living, where they are frequently "caught up in a cycle of expensive, self-indulgent habits."[29] The paltry financial rewards of most street crimes would discourage most members of the middle class from choosing such behaviors. However, when coupled with other intrinsic rewards of crime—such as status, autonomy, and action— these rewards may be enough to turn the heads of many.

In addition to studying the factors that contribute to one's decision to become involved in and continue with crime (referred to as "involvement decisions"), rational choice theorists advocate the modeling of criminal "event decisions," which include the practical aspects of selecting targets, enacting the crime, and disposing of stolen goods. Ethnographic research that examines event decisions suggests that offenders have developed a portfolio of skills that aids in the successful completion of crime. Robbers have specific patterns for how to approach victims, announce the crime, separate goods from victims, and make their escape.[30] Likewise, burglars have specific techniques for assessing whether or not residents are home, entering houses, and searching for goods.[31] What these and similar studies show is that offenders use experience to script their crimes to increase their chances of being successful, and that these scripts vary by the type of crime involved.[32]

When applied in criminology, rational choice theory provides a framework to guide thinking about crime and its prevention. As such, the theory provides a tool for modeling the various decisions that offenders make at each stage of their crimes. This perspective places greater weight on situational variables that influence not only criminal dispositions but also discrete crime events.[33] Prior to this development, criminological theories focused mainly on the social paths that lead people to criminality and completely ignored the contexts of the actual crime. A framework that can account for both crime and criminality can have great explanatory power. Modeling decisions using this framework accords an increased understanding of how the situations and circumstances under which highly specific forms of crime occur can be manipulated to reduce criminal opportunities and make crime riskier.[34]

THE STRUCTURE OF THIS BOOK

The central purpose of this study is to explore the decision-making processes of identity thieves. Before tackling this issue, we provide readers with a profile of identity thieves. Chapter 1 presents a detailed description of our sample and compares it with those available in other research on the topic. We also provide brief biographies of a handful of offenders, tracing their initiation into identity theft and describing how they carried out their crimes, their downfall, and their eventual incarceration.

After giving readers a sense of who identity thieves are and what they do, we shift our focus to answering an important question: Why do people choose to engage in identity theft? As we will discover in chapter 2, the answers are obvious, yet at the same time complicated. Our discussion illuminates the reasons provided by offenders and explores how lifestyles influence decisions. While "money" is the primary reason given for their crimes, we examine what criminals do with that money. We also should not forget that sometimes the motives people provide for their actions are not without their own motives. Therefore, we discuss the ways in which identity thieves justify and excuse their participation in these acts.

Chapter 3 turns to the various organizational schemes used to carry out identity theft and the organizational alignment of networks and roles. Such schemes include three principal types: loners, occupational teams, and street-level identity theft (SLIT) rings. In our discussion, we elaborate on the specific techniques used by identity thieves to locate victims' personal information and convert it into cash or goods. We also discuss the advantages and disadvantages, from the offender's perspective, of each form of organization.

In addition to understanding the rewards of crime, it is also important to understand the risks of such behavior and how offenders overcome these risks. These factors are examined in chapter 4. Identity thieves indicate that, for the most part, they do not dwell on the potential risks of their enterprises. We describe the reasons they provide for their lack of fear, either for getting caught or for the consequences of arrest. We also present the strategies that identity thieves employ to avoid being detected by victims and law enforcement, along with the skills they develop as they persist in their crimes. The chapter concludes with a discussion of the accuracy of their risk assessments.

In the final chapter, we provide an overview of what we have learned about identity theft and identity thieves and our thoughts on controlling such crime. Here we discuss the implications our findings have for developing and expanding rational choice theory. Specifically, we focus on implications for better understanding criminal persistence. In addition, our description of identity thieves' accounts of their crimes has implications for crime control, especially situational crime prevention.

A methodological appendix rounds out the book. We recognize that samples like ours are subject to criticism; thus, we provide great detail into how we located participants and how we elicited information from them. We hope readers come away with a better understanding of how identity thieves become involved in their crimes, how they go about their day-to-day tasks, and how we can reduce the prevalence of this crime.

||||||||| 1 |||||||||

PROFILES

The paucity of research on identity theft, coupled with the low arrest rate of identity thieves, has made it difficult to form a clear picture of the "typical" offender. What type of person steals someone else's identity and uses it for personal gain? Does a typical profile of an identity thief even exist? Are they similar to other white-collar criminals, or are they more akin to street criminals involved in scams, property crimes, and the sale of illegal drugs?

As it turns out, the answers to these questions are complicated. Our research shows that identity thieves are a heterogeneous group who hail from all walks of life. Their family backgrounds, educational attainments, work histories, and criminal histories run the gamut from poverty to wealth, less than a high school education to graduate degrees, and from no prior arrests to incarcerations for everything from fraud to violent crime.

Consider the characteristics of the identity thieves profiled in the following three news stories, published within a year of each other. In August 2009, Albert Gonzalez, the twenty-eight-year-old son of Cuban immigrants, made national news for his arrest in what prosecutors labeled "the single largest hacking and identity theft case ever prosecuted."[1] According to authorities, Gonzalez and his associates, two of whom were alleged Russian hackers, attacked the databases of several major retailers, including 7-Eleven, Heartland Payment Systems, which processes payments for more than 250,000 businesses, and Hannaford Brothers, a Maine-based supermarket chain. It is estimated that over 130 million credit and debit card numbers were stolen using a sophisticated hacking technique. The stolen information was uploaded onto servers controlled by Gonzalez (who was known online as the "Soupnazi" hacker) and his associates. The data were then sold to others, mainly Eastern European bulk buyers, who used it to make fraudulent purchases and unauthorized withdrawals from banks.

Six months later, in February 2010, Sharon Seeley made headlines when she was sentenced to thirty-four years in a Texas prison for her role in the identity thefts of over three thousand current and former teachers in the Irving (Texas) Independent School District. Seeley, a forty-year-old single mother of one, claimed that she found a binder containing employees' personal information, such as names, addresses, and social security numbers, in a dumpster owned by the school district. She used the information to apply for credit cards and racked up thousands of dollars in charges in her victims' names. At sentencing, Seeley explained to the judge that she turned to identity theft to fund her addiction to methamphetamine and to support her daughter.[2]

Not long after Seeley's thefts, Adrienne Toney, an employee of the City of New York Parks and Recreation Department, was arrested for fraudulent use of stolen social security numbers. According to federal prosecutors, an individual supplied Toney with the names and social security numbers of at least ten individuals, which she then used to forge letters on her home computer. The letters purported to be from the Social Security Administration, acknowledging receipt of requests for replacement social security cards. Toney printed the fraudulent letters on the city-owned printer at the recreation center where she worked, then sold the letters to the person who had supplied her with the names and social security numbers. The letters were used to obtain other government-issued identification documents, such as driver's licenses, passports, and birth certificates. A few months earlier, two other New York City employees also were arrested and sentenced for stealing and selling information to the same individual to whom Toney sold the false letters. One was a former employee of the Human Resource Administration, who sold copies of welfare recipients' birth certificates and social security cards, the other a former employee of the Bureau of Vital Statistics, who stole and sold parental identification obtained from birth certificates. Toney had worked for the Parks and Recreation Department for four years

when she was arrested. She had been hired as a job training participant under the department's Opportunity Program, established to
"encourage future employment through the development of basic
skills for vulnerable New Yorkers."[3]

On the surface, Albert Gonzalez, Sharon Seeley, and Adrienne
Toney have very little in common. According to information provided by various media accounts and legal documents, they differ
by race, class, educational achievement, and occupational history.
They are three very different people with very different backgrounds, yet they share one thing in common: they have all been
labeled as identity thieves. And unlike most street offenders, their
crimes were deemed serious enough to warrant attention by the
news media. From the cyberthief working in collusion with Rus-
sians to hack into corporate databases, to the methamphetamine
addict stealing identities out of dumpsters to fund her habit, to
the government employee working with other employees to steal
information and use it to obtain fraudulent documents, these
identity thieves' methods are far from uniform. The diversity in
their stories illustrates the difficulty in profiling the "typical" identity thief.

It is true that profiling any specific group of criminals from
media accounts is complicated, as the media is biased in favor
of "sensational" stories. The difficulty in profiling identity thieves
is compounded by the lack of reliable data on them. We simply
don't have enough information about those who are most likely
to perpetrate the crime. In fact, outside of the current study, there
have been no systematic attempts, either by survey or interview,
to collect data directly from identity thieves. What little is known
about these offenders is based on data collected from police reports, closed case files of various law enforcement agencies, or
newspaper articles.[4] The results of these studies reveal some similarities in a number of areas, including the gender, age, race, and
employment status of offenders, as well as the methods thieves use
to acquire information. In general, these studies show a group of
offenders for which the majority are male, in their early to mid-
thirties, black, and unemployed.[5] This group also tends to rely on

low-tech methods of acquiring their victims' information, such as dumpster diving, theft of mail, or through the offender's place of work (if employed).

Researchers have used these existing data sources to create typologies that categorize the ways identity thieves steal information and convert it into cash or goods. Some have suggested that identity thieves can be classified into three groups: situational, routine, and professional.[6] Situational offenders are those who come across personal information, usually through legitimate activity (in their jobs, for example), then misuse this information for their own benefit, either directly or by selling it to others. These offenders typically are responding to temporary pressures and participate in crime only for a short time. Routine offenders, on the other hand, have prolonged careers in crime and often take on employment at multiple locations to facilitate their illegal activities. Professional thieves are the most sophisticated of the three types. They often work in criminal organizations whose members have individual roles. While fewer in number than the other two types, professional thieves are responsible for more elaborate and costly crimes.

Another system for classifying identity thieves, based on the offenders' levels of sophistication, was developed from a content analysis of identity theft stories published in U.S. newspapers from 1995 to 2005.[7] Four categories, ranging from very simple to complex international ring networks, emerged from the data. The first, "circumstantial identity theft," is rather simple, involves little planning, and is often the result of environmental circumstance. Sharon Seeley fits this group well. A majority of the sample (51 percent) was classified as "general identity theft," which involves a greater level of sophistication than the circumstantial type. This type of offender purposely seeks out opportunities to steal victims' information, and the crime involves increased levels of planning, organization, premeditation, and effort. Offenders who engage in "sophisticated identity theft" use a variety of tactics to steal from a large number of victims on a national or global scale. Some make extensive use of technology, including the Internet, while others use simpler methods to steal identifying information and convert that information to goods or money. Thefts that involve even higher levels of organization and complexity were classified as "highly sophisticated identity theft." These identity thieves typically make extensive use of technology and often operate as a team. They fit the stereotype of sophisticated hackers who steal identities online, much like Albert Gonzalez.

While the demographic profiles that emerge from these studies are generally similar to the results of our research, we delve deeper: exploring offenders' backgrounds and lifestyles, their methods of organization, and the ways in which they assess the rewards and risks of their crimes. The portrait of identity thieves that emerges from our study is more detailed than any in the previous literature and suggests that straightforward classification will not be a simple task. The range of personal histories and methods of stealing information are as diverse as the narratives of the men and women we interviewed.

CHARACTERISTICS OF THE SAMPLE

To determine the backgrounds of the offenders in our sample, we inquired about various demographic characteristics, including age, race, gender, employment status, and educational achievement. We also asked offenders about their socioeconomic status, family status, and criminal history, including prior arrests, convictions, and drug use.[8] Overall, we found that our sample came from all walks of life and had diverse criminal histories. In fact, they were just as likely to resemble persistent street thieves (hustlers, burglars, or low-level drug dealers, for example) as middle-class fraudsters (such as embezzlers). In the following descriptions, we rely on offenders' own words to add context to the simple frequencies typically presented in ethnographic research.[9]

Demographics and Family Background

Our sample of fifty-nine inmates included twenty-three men and thirty-six women. This of course does not mean that women are more likely to commit identity theft than men are, nor are they more likely to be incarcerated than men. In fact, of the nearly five hundred identity thieves we were able to locate, 63 percent were male and 37 percent were female. The gender discrepancy in our sample is likely due to our sampling strategy and the higher response rate from female inmates. Most of the people we interviewed were born and raised in the United States. Four were born in other countries, although all had spent several years in the United States prior to their arrest and incarceration. The age of participants at the time of their interviews ranged from twenty-three to sixty, with a mean age of thirty-eight. The racial makeup of the sample was 44 percent white, 53 percent black, and 3 percent other.[10]

To gain a better understanding of their life experiences, we asked offenders to describe what their life was like growing up. Approximately 39 percent were raised in single-parent households, typically headed by their mother or another female relative, such as a grandmother or aunt. The remaining 61 percent came from two-parent households. The women in our sample were more likely to have been raised in intact families: 45 percent of women versus 36 percent of men.

We used a subjective measure to assess social class, asking offenders to self-identify based on their parents' occupations and lifestyles and on their current assessments of where they stood socially and economically. When asked to describe their family's status while growing up, most offenders classified their family background as either working class or middle/upper-middle class, 48 percent and 42 percent, respectively. Of those who self-defined as working class, a few reported that their parents made a living through crime, but the majority said that their parents had jobs, such as manual laborer, for example. When asked what their families were like, Jamie's response is typical of those claiming working-class status: "My mother works and my father is in the army. It was a working class family. [Growing up] we were the average family. . . . I had a real good childhood. It wasn't like . . . this really horrible childhood."

Almost half the sample claimed to hail from financially comfortable families. The parents of these offenders held jobs as doctors, nurses, engineers, or other white-collar positions. When asked to describe her childhood, Lois said, "Typical middle-class. . . . My mother didn't work until the children were grown and out of the house (I have two younger sisters). My father's always been in law enforcement; he's also military—he's a colonel in the army." Debbie reported, "[My] parents went to work and we went to school. . . . We did our chores. We had company every now and then. We had computers. Pretty much didn't want for anything."

The gender breakdown of class shows that female offenders were significantly more likely to claim middle-class or upper-middle-class upbringings than the men. For females, 50 percent self-reported middle-class backgrounds, while 41 percent reported lower or working-class backgrounds. For males, 30 percent claimed middle-class backgrounds, while 52 percent reported a lower-class upbringing.

Familial Status

Most offenders were currently married or had been married previously: 27 percent married, 35 percent separated/divorced, and 5 percent widowed. The remaining 33 percent had never been married. Ten members of the sample listed divorce or separation, among many other reasons, for instigating identity theft. Emma's remarks characterized this process:

> I had gotten divorced, I was a single mom, and I was struggling. I was working, but I've worked for a number of years as an independent contractor doing medical transcription and I lost some of my accounts. I was struggling with depression and dealing with a lot of things. I had met some ladies and we started talking and . . . we began to socialize and they said, "We do identity theft and we think you would do really good going into a bank and taking some money out. We can split that with you and you can have some money." I said okay and that's how I started.

Only one individual said that her thefts led to her divorce. Approximately 75 percent of offenders had children.

Educational Attainment and Work Histories

The educational accomplishments of our sample of identity thieves were generally in line with those of the wider U.S. population. As a group they were relatively well educated. Almost 53 percent had some college or a college degree, 17 percent had a high school diploma, and 15 percent had less than a high school degree. Several offenders had earned post-baccalaureate degrees, including a few with law degrees, and one with a master's degree in computer science.[11]

Most offenders, both men and women, had been employed at some point during their lifetimes. Their jobs included day laborers, store clerks, nurses, and attorneys. At the time of their crimes, 53 percent were employed. About thirty-six percent of the sample reported that their employment facilitated their identity thefts. The majority of those who used their jobs to carry out their crimes committed mortgage fraud. Others worked at organizations that allowed them access to credit card numbers or social security numbers (for example, a department store that granted credit or a government agency). Bradley worked as a junior recruiter for the National Guard. In his words:

> The military has [a form], which has all of your history on it, social security numbers, dates of birth, last known addresses, that kind of stuff. And we use that to solicit people to come into the National Guard. . . . After I had gotten out [of the National Guard] I still had the information. . . . I had talked to some other people about how to get credit cards and stuff like that. Then I started.

While not all of the offenders we interviewed said that they accessed and stole information from their place of employment, some of them did use their positions to facilitate identity theft. Such offenders typically claimed that they legitimately sought employment at these organizations, then were approached by others to commit fraud. Few said that they sought employment for the sole purpose of gaining easy access to sensitive information or to facilitate identity thefts. It was much more common for women to use their employment to facilitate their crimes than it was for men.

Whereas only a quarter of the men in our sample made such use of their jobs, almost half of the women did so. This difference is likely a reflection of the gendered nature of occupations, as the women in our sample were disproportionately employed in real estate and related occupations.

Arrest and Conviction Histories

The majority of the identity thieves we interviewed (63 percent) had been arrested multiple times for crimes other than those for which they were currently incarcerated. Most of the prior arrests were for financial fraud or identity theft (n = 26), but drug use/sales (n = 11) and property crimes (n = 13) were also relatively common. Forty-four percent also had been convicted of a crime. Men were more likely to have previous convictions than were women. Again, most of these convictions were for financial fraud or identity theft (n = 15). Whereas fraud was the most frequently committed crime for which both males and females were convicted, only one female was convicted of a previous identity theft.

It is unclear as to the degree that offenders specialize in particular crimes. Here again our sample showed diversity. Prior arrest patterns indicate that a large portion of participants had engaged in various types of crime, including drug, property, and violent crimes. Yet, the majority of participants claimed that they only committed identity thefts or comparable frauds (such as check fraud). While several offenders described having committed other crimes in the past, they stopped these other criminal endeavors because they could make more money through identity theft. For example, Bridgette said, "[selling drugs is] not the answer. That's not where the money is."

Substance Use Histories

We also questioned inmates about their prior drug use. Fifty-eight percent had tried drugs. The most commonly used drugs were marijuana, cocaine in various forms, and methamphetamine.

Thirty-eight percent reported having been addicted to their drug of choice; less than one-third of males but two-fifths of females admitted being addicted. For both male and female participants, addictions to methamphetamine and cocaine (in powder or crack forms) were the most frequently mentioned. Of those offenders who said that they were using drugs while committing identity theft, the majority claimed that their indulgence did not contribute to their crimes. Bruce's response represented a typical claim. In his words, "I mean there was some drug use and people I knew but I don't think that actually ever fueled what they were doing. Especially at the identity theft level that I was doing it at, or they were doing it at, [it] had really nothing to do with drugs."

Twenty-four percent reported that drug use contributed to their identity thefts; women were slightly more likely than men to admit that addiction contributed to their crimes. When asked if drugs influenced his decision to engage in identity theft, Jay answered emphatically, "Absolutely. One hundred percent." Despite current claims about the link between methamphetamines and identity theft, only 8 percent of those with whom we spoke said that methamphetamine use directly contributed to their crimes.

OFFENDER BIOGRAPHIES

The diverse backgrounds and lifestyles reflected in the summary data represent some of the most interesting discoveries of our research. While aggregate data are useful for understanding what offenders are like in general, they do not tell us how these factors influence the choices that offenders make; they don't tell us how identity thieves carry out their acts, nor why they choose to commit the crime. One of the advantages of speaking directly to offenders is that they can provide their own reasons, in their own words; they can explain why they continue to commit crime in the face of risk, and describe how they see themselves as people. By presenting the offenders' voices alongside our own analyses, we gain a deeper understanding of the decision-making processes of identity thieves. Although the details of the lives and crimes of those we interviewed will come in the following pages, we first present brief biographies of several of our participants. These biographies again highlight the diversity of identity thieves in our sample.

Lawrence

Lawrence is a self-defined "hustler" who came to identity theft through a network of street thieves and con men. He was born in Jacksonville, Florida, to an alcoholic father and a mother who was twenty years his father's junior. His father was married to another woman when Lawrence and his twin brother were born; after a few years, their mother moved the boys and their sister to a religious compound in Alabama. Lawrence described the church as a "religious cult" that used physical abuse to enforce discipline. At the age of fourteen, he contacted his father, who still lived in Florida, to plan his "escape." After getting away from the compound, Lawrence moved in with his father. His father gained custody of Lawrence and his twin brother after their mother, who refused to leave the church, failed to show up for the custody hearing. At the time, his father was going through a divorce, which left the family in serious financial trouble. Eventually, his father filed for bankruptcy, obtained a second mortgage on the house, and took a job driving trucks across the country.

Lawrence's description of his high school years illustrates the role his father's financial situation played in his self-perceived path toward criminal behavior.

> I was like fifteen or sixteen in the house by myself, so things were getting pretty bad. They come around, cut the lights off and stuff like that. I was trying to stay in school and I had to get a job. That job wasn't working out because I wasn't making enough money because I was working part-time because I was young. I couldn't pay for the lights and stuff like that. [My father] was gone coast to coast. He would never send any money home to me. I started selling a lot of stuff in the house to keep food in and to try to keep the light bills paid and stuff like that. Things got way out of hand.

One of Lawrence's teachers, in an attempt to help, got him a part-time job conducting phone surveys for a credit card company. His job involved calling customers to ask them questions about their accounts. After a short time Lawrence recognized the opportunity for fraud and began to use customers' information to list additional cardholders (his friends) on their accounts.

> I had all the information on the computer, so I just started getting their names and stuff. Going home, ordering credit cards and putting their name, and send them to a fake residence to get the credit cards that way. What I'd do is I'd put somebody else's name as the additional cardholder and when I get the cards back, I'd give that person a card, and I'd just charge. [He would] give me just a thousand out of it or something and he'd keep the rest.

Lawrence's life turned further toward crime when he was recruited into an identity theft ring. He found these crimes more profitable than his own credit card scams. As well as paying the bills, he spent his new income on marijuana, cocaine, strip clubs, and girlfriends. His involvement in drugs and his association with other criminals led to several arrests and his identity as a "hustler." Eventually, Lawrence branched out on his own, creating a team— including his father and twin brother—who committed identity theft and check fraud. A typical crime involved buying identifying information from prostitutes, who stole it from clients, or from friends, who would steal information from the homes of girlfriends or acquaintances. Lawrence explained how his hustler identity and his street connections enabled him to acquire information for a relatively low price:

> See once you on the streets, you run across prostitutes and stuff like that. Prostitutes have a way of working, doing their thing, and it be going in a person's pocket to get whatever they want to out of a person's pocket. Dude got a girlfriend and his girlfriend's parents, they own their own business or whatever, and they stay in the upscale houses and stuff, nice neighborhoods. Of course I would pay him like one hundred, two hundred dollars for that. But somebody that stay in the projects, fifty dollars, twenty-five dollars.

After buying a victim's information, Lawrence would find a "player" to pose as the victim and withdraw money from the victim's bank account. He described a typical transaction like this: "There's a lot of ways you can do it. Say that the person already got an existing account. I would teach [my partner] how to do the signature. I would let him do it a couple of times; let him practice on it. Then once I feel like he got it down pat, I send them in there and let them cash checks in that person's name. Just deposit the money and withdraw whatever."

Lawrence's crimes continued for several years, until a former friend (and coconspirator in some identity thefts) was arrested for an unrelated crime. In an attempt to get a shorter sentence, he turned Lawrence over to the authorities. Lawrence and his brother were arrested by federal agents. He was convicted and sentenced to three years in federal prison. Shortly after his release, Lawrence returned to his old habits and was arrested again. He was convicted of fraud and at the time of this writing was serving time in a low-security federal prison.

Bruce

Bruce was an identity thief who had little or no connections to other thieves. He acted alone and outwardly portrayed the image of white, middle-class respectability. He was born in Indiana, but moved with his parents to Florida after a state conviction for fraud when he was nineteen. Because his father worked as an executive for a car company and his mother owned her own insurance company, he lived a happy and very comfortable life. Ironically, Bruce attributes his downfall to his privileged upbringing. In his own words:

> My parents had a lot of credit at the time. They were kind of upper middle class. So we had a bit of money and I was constantly using it. Even before sixteen I was using their credit cards. And I was used to using credit cards and I don't think I really understood that they had to be paid for at that time or whatever. So even at that age I would just take their credit card or whatever out of my father's wallet or my mother's purse and then purchase what I wanted and just put it back. And I think from that point on there was never any problem with it really. They'd ask me, "What did you buy? When did I tell you that you could buy that?" Stuff like that. Other than that I didn't get into too much trouble for it.

After graduating from high school, Bruce enrolled in a state university. During this time, he took a part-time job as a "credit and collection manager" at a furniture store. The job taught him how credit bureaus work and allowed him access to customers' credit information. Working at the furniture store helped him realize that he could earn more money by misusing customers' information than he could as an employee. In an attempt to maintain his accustomed lifestyle—to which he thought he was entitled—he began to use customers' information to obtain credit cards, open bank accounts, and secure mortgages and motor vehicle loans. This phase of his criminal career was short-lived; he was caught and convicted soon after his first few thefts. Despite this early conviction, Bruce embarked on a fifteen-year career of identity theft. He became quite prolific and maintained a lavish lifestyle, all the while hiding his crimes from friends and family.

During his long criminal career, Bruce used many methods of stealing information. One involved stealing mail from the residents of quiet suburban neighborhoods. He would walk through a neighborhood placing flyers in mailboxes, while at the same time sifting through residents' mail and pulling out envelopes that might contain personally identifying information. He especially desired bank and credit card statements, doctor's bills, and any other mail that would likely reveal the owner's date of birth, social security number, or account numbers. Armed with this information, Bruce would return home and pull credit reports on his victims, using their complete financial histories to ascertain whether they suited his definition of a "good identity." If they met his criteria—good credit, stable residence, no children—he ordered credit cards in the owners' names, applied for home and car loans, and deposited credit card checks in their bank accounts, then withdrew the money. Bruce used the proceeds from his crimes to live a self-indulgent life, buying homes in the most desirable cities in the United States, purchasing fast cars and designer clothing, and traveling around the world.

According to Bruce, he was caught when he deviated from his rule to never use a friend's personal information. The friend discovered that a credit card account had been opened in his name and promptly reported the fraud to authorities. During the investigation, FBI agents tracked checks written on the account back to Bruce. He was arrested, convicted, and sentenced to nine years and seven months in federal prison, followed by five years of supervised release. At the time of this writing he was finishing his sentence at a low-security facility.

Joel

The oldest of seven children, Joel was five when his parents separated. His father worked as a dispatcher for a taxi company and his mother was a nurse. Joel said he began his criminal career at the age of thirteen when he called in a bomb threat to school. Although today such behavior would likely lead to serious consequences, for Joel it resulted only in a one-day suspension. While growing up, he had been heavily involved in the use of illegal drugs, claiming that he was twelve when he first used LSD laced with amphetamines. He described how his mother's use of amphetamines to control her weight and his extended family's participation in the manufacturing of methamphetamine exposed him to drugs.

> My mother used to get big jugs of Benzedrine and Dexedrine back then. She'd go to the doctor and the doctor would give her a quart jug full for her diet. So I started doing them. I started injecting amphetamines when I was seventeen. I come from an area where this crystal meth was huge when I was young. I mean, I come from a family of brothers and cousins who manufactured it.

Around the same time, Joel became involved with check kiting.[12] "From the time I was eighteen I had my own checking account," he reported. "And at eighteen you just write checks whenever you want to. I was married at that time and had a child, so I would just write checks for whatever, whether there was money in the bank or not. From that point on, I was involved with checks."

Joel's experience with check kiting eventually led to his participation in identity theft. His methods involved a simple yet creative way of inducing victims to divulge their personal information. Joel

would place an advertisement in a local newspaper, seeking applicants for positions at a "new" company in the area. The advertisement would have all the contents of a legitimate help-wanted ad,
including a description of the job requirements and, perhaps more
enticingly, the "excellent" medical and dental benefits the company
would provide to its employees after just ninety days on the job.
Joel would set up an "employment site" in a rented hotel confer-
ence room; when the first female applicant arrived, he would offer
her a job immediately and task her with accepting applications. Joel
would then leave for the day. The application forms included the
standard requests for name, address, phone number, and employment experience, along with space for the applicant's social security
number and photograph. At the end of the day, Joel would return
to collect the applications and evaluate the victim pool. With the
help of the attached photographs, he would select the applications
of those who shared his physical appearance (sex, hair color, eye
color, and race/ethnicity), then shred the rest. Unfortunately for the
chosen applicants, the information they provided would be used
to create counterfeit social security cards and birth certificates, to
apply for driver's licenses and, eventually, to open bank accounts
from which to pilfer. After exhausting the potential of each round's
victims, Joel would set up an employment site in another city.

Over the course of his criminal career, Joel continued his drug
use, earned a bachelor's degree in computer science, got married
twice, and fathered three children. He was eventually incarcerated
for bank fraud but escaped from a federal facility. While on the run
with his wife and children, he used identity theft to fund his travels.
His crime spree ended three years later, at age fifty-two, when he
was arrested by federal authorities after a nationwide manhunt and
a profile on *America's Most Wanted*. He was sentenced to eleven
years and eight months in federal prison.

Kendra

Kendra grew up in foster care in Seattle, Washington. At the
age of eight, she and her sister were adopted by a family with two

other adopted children and three biological children. One of her adoptive parents owned a manufacturing company; the other was a psychiatrist. Although she was part of a caring family, Kendra never felt like she fit in: "I hear a lot of adopted kids do have problems with the family or something. I guess in my case it might be true because I can't seem to click with my family for nothing in the world. They come visit me here [in prison], they help me, but I don't know." Her lack of attachment to her family was perhaps a contributing factor to her early involvement in street gangs, drug use and drug selling, and property crimes.

Upon completing high school, she enrolled in a local community college. After completing one year, she transferred to another community college, then dropped out. Kendra had married a police officer when she was seventeen. That marriage lasted almost six years and produced a daughter who lives with her father. Her second marriage was to a native of Saudi Arabia. At twenty-six, Kendra gave birth to another daughter, with whom she has had little contact since her husband returned to Saudi Arabia, taking the child with him.

Kendra's legitimate work history included a six-month stint at a computer company. In contrast, her criminal history was lengthier and more varied. She used and sold drugs (mainly marijuana), admitted to committing burglary and shoplifting, and spent two years in state prison for assault with a gun on a police officer. Kendra's participation in identity theft began at the age of twenty-seven and continued for almost six years until she was arrested, convicted, and incarcerated.

During her career as an identity thief, Kendra worked with a boyfriend and eight others in a ring of identity thieves. In some cases, her boyfriend entered people's homes and stole the owners' personal information; in other cases, ring members purchased information from street hustlers involved in drug use and selling, pickpocketing, or burglary. Kendra's main task was creating the identification documents needed to cash checks and apply for store credit cards. She had the software and equipment to produce driver's licenses, which were used to apply for store credit and to cash checks at the victims' banks. If the thieves obtained a victim's social security number, they opened new credit card accounts. Kendra even managed to secure a mortgage for the condominium in which she and her boyfriend lived. Kendra and her accomplices were caught when one of their ring members turned informant for the local police after his arrest on drug charges. When we interviewed Kendra, she was awaiting sentencing for her crimes. She eventually served over four years in a federal camp for women.

Tameka

Tameka lived with her mother and sister in Birmingham, Alabama. Her mother worked at a hospital until she began seeing a man who would eventually lead her into a life of drugs and frequent incarcerations. As a result, Tameka and her sister moved out of project housing into a home with her grandmother and two uncles. When her grandmother left the home to reunite with a husband she hadn't seen in thirty years, Tameka and her sister were left alone with their uncles. At this time, one uncle began sexually assaulting Tameka. The abuse lasted for two years. At age ten, Tameka ran away; for the next several years, she was in and out of juvenile facilities. She was incarcerated in state prison when she was sixteen and released two years later, in the mid-1990s.

At the time of her release, Tameka reported that "pimps and prostitutes was the big thing. And this one guy wanted me to prostitute for him and I told him no I didn't do that, my family boosted [shoplifted] and sold drugs and stuff, that was the big thing then. So I wasn't gonna never be caught dead [prostituting]." After refusing to engage in prostitution, she fled to New York to live with her mother, who had since moved there. Tameka claimed that she had not used drugs before this time. In the following passage, she describes what happened next.

> When I got to New York, the first night I got there my mom had me drugged. I was never a drug user, my friends smoked marijuana and all that stuff but I never got into the thing. . . . When my mother gave me drugs I thought well if I do this, she'll accept me,

because I never had that kind of attention from her. So she gave
me drugs for the first time and I end up being up there and, she
was strung out really bad, and me and her got into it [about her
new husband]. And she turned against me for him. Then one guy
that I stayed with most of the time (I was there like five years) he
fed me drugs day in day out and I end up going to prison three or
four times back to back. I've been to prison three times in New
York and had my first three kids up there.

Tameka's drug use led to connections to other street hustlers,
including Robert, the man who would become her husband and
father to one of her five children. These individuals were involved
in property crimes, credit card frauds, and identity theft. After numerous stints in state and federal prisons, Tameka left her husband
and moved with her children to the home of a female friend. She
found a legitimate job but did not sever all ties with her husband
until her most recent incarceration.

During the period when Tameka was actively engaged in crime,
she and Robert worked together with several other "employees" to
steal identities and use the information to open accounts and cash
checks. Their typical theft began by purchasing information from
an employee of a downtown bank, including cancelled checks.
Robert would bring that material to Tameka, who would compile a
list of names and account numbers, then return it to Robert, who
in turn would pass the list to a rogue employee at a credit bureau.
That person would access the victims' credit reports and supply
Robert with their dates of birth, home addresses, and social security numbers. Using a digital camera, laptop, and license-making
machine—purchased from an employee at the company that pro-
duces such machines for the state's department of motor vehicles—
Tameka would create driver's licenses from the stolen information.
Some of the licenses would contain Tameka's picture, some would
feature the pictures of others in their "organization," referred to
as "runners," primarily poor young women Robert recruited from
strip clubs and other places. After checking the victims' account
balances, Tameka and the runners would travel to up to three bank
branches per day, for three consecutive days, withdrawing money

from the victims' accounts. While some of the money was squirreled away for the future, most of the proceeds from these illicit activities were spent quickly on alcohol, drugs, and partying.

The stress of this lifestyle led Tameka to give up crime and start a legitimate business. Unfortunately for her, federal agents did not give up investigating her prior frauds; she was eventually arrested and convicted for identity theft. When we spoke with Tameka, she was serving sixty-three months in federal prison. After her release, she moved back to Alabama, where by all indications she has desisted from crime.

Abbey

The middle child of five girls, Abbey grew up in a single-parent household in Chicago. Her parents divorced when she was four years old, due to her father's repeated physical abuse of her mother. Abbey's family situation did not improve when her mother remarried; that man sexually abused Abbey at age twelve. After graduating from high school, Abbey got her first job and began to take classes at a local community college. Later, she decided that college wasn't for her and began hanging out "with the wrong type of friends." After traveling for a while, she eventually landed in Florida at age twenty-two and took a job signing up college students for credit card accounts. While working for the credit card company, Abbey met a coworker, fell in love, and got married.

Abbey's marriage began to dissolve when she found out that her husband had cheated on her just two months into their marriage. Although devastated, she decided to stay with her husband and "really try to build a family because I made a pact in my head when I was little that I will never get divorced, ever." She gave birth to their son and they remained together for two more years, until she kicked her husband out of the house. Abbey took a job at a small mortgage company, co-owned by a husband-and-wife team. She eventually returned to her husband and landed a new job at a different mortgage company. It was here that she was introduced to large-scale mortgage fraud using stolen identities.

During the first few months at her new job, Abbey simply put together mortgage applications with documents given to her by her boss. Later, she was presented with an opportunity to earn $250,000 by posing as a home buyer. A mortgage broker in the company wanted to "punish" an acquaintance for an incident involving vandalism to the home of the broker's fiancé. Using the acquaintance's personal information, Abbey helped assemble a loan application and secured a driver's license with her own photograph but in the victim's name. When the mortgage closed, Abbey picked up the check, opened a bank account, and deposited the funds. The plan was to withdraw the money after waiting the required three days for the check to clear. The bank did not honor the check, however, and after several attempts to withdraw the money from other branches, Abbey quit. She was arrested five months later and eventually sentenced to serve two years in federal prison.

◆   ◆   ◆

The brief biographies presented here reveal the array of life-styles, backgrounds, and operating methods found among identity thieves. As readers can see, the identity thieves we spoke with came from all walks of life and appear to share only a single common denominator—the crime. In the following chapters, we present identity theft from the viewpoint of those who likely know the most about it: the thieves themselves. Our goal is to present the lived experiences of identity thieves, including how they organize to carry out the act, how they assess the risks and rewards of the crime, and how this information can be used to develop more effective policy to ward off future victimizations.

||||||||| **2** |||||||||

WHY THEY STEAL

It is not unreasonable to assume that many of us have contemplated committing a crime at some point in our lives. We may have visualized taking a coveted toy from a friend's home, or stealing a candy bar our mother refused to buy from the grocery store. We may have even contemplated seizing opportunities for more serious forms of crime that, at least on the surface, appeared to be highly rewarding and risk free. Undoubtedly, the ease with which one can access other peoples' personally identifying information has made many typically law-abiding citizens think they too could easily profit from a stolen identity. Fortunately, most have not succumbed to these temptations. Why do some people ignore the moral and legal proscriptions against using the personal information of others to commit fraud? Why did Joel set up fake employment sites to trick people into divulging sensitive data, then use that information to defraud banks? Why did Bruce steal mail then obtain credit cards in other people's names?

When researchers seek to understand what motivates people to commit crime, it is not uncommon for them to let offenders speak for themselves. Through their own words, offenders can provide a potentially illuminating explanation of why they did what they did. Unfortunately, previous investigations of identity theft have not sought such information; instead, they have inferred motivations from stories told by victims and law enforcement agents. For the most part, this research suggests that identity thieves are motivated by a desire for money, to remain hidden from authorities, or to avoid purchasing utilities and other services in their own names. Although these explanations are accurate, they merely skim the surface of offenders' motivations. They do not tell us why offenders choose identity theft when they have a variety of ways to fulfill their desires. If they seek money, why not get it through legitimate means? If set on illegally obtaining money, why not some other offense? We suggest that those who choose identity theft do so because they see it as inherently rewarding—both financially and phenomenologically—and that they are able to justify or excuse their actions in a way that successfully maintains a positive self-image. For those we interviewed, other modes of obtaining money did not offer such advantages.

TANGIBLE REWARDS: MONEY

For offenders in general, the simple answer for why they choose to engage in crime is the desire for quick and easy money.[1] The identity thieves we spoke with certainly did not contradict the claim that money is the primary incentive for their crimes. Identity theft can be richly rewarding. Indeed, it provides what Carlos described as a "shitload of money." Lawrence probably best articulated the financial motivation: "[Identity theft] is all about the money. That's all it's about. It's all about the money. If there ain't no money, it don't make sense." In fact, the ease with which they could secure money led many to give up other criminal endeavors to specialize in identity theft. Dale, who switched from burglaries to identity theft, claimed that, "[Identity theft] is easier and you get the money, you know. You get a lot of money." When asked why she quit selling drugs, Sylvia, a female street hustler, said, "that's not the answer. That's not where the money is." For her, identity theft was simply easier than remaining in the drug game. Gladys recalled why she stopped shoplifting to focus on identity theft:

> Being arrested at [a department store] scared the mess out of me. I know if I ever get in trouble there I'll do a lot of time. So I left [shoplifting] completely alone. And when I learned of [identity theft], it's a piece of cake and it's one lump sum of money. I can make like two thousand dollars in three days. Just go open an account one day, they send the card in three days, and you get the money the next day.

Offenders used different methods to profit from stolen identities, with a corresponding variation in their income. Dustin, who used stolen identities to cash counterfeit checks, explained, "I'll put it to you like this, forging checks, counterfeiting checks in an hour—depending on the proximity of the banks that you're working—I have made seven thousand dollars in one hour." Russell said, "[Identity theft] was the only type of crime that I did because fraud paid more money than anything. I could go out on a good day, do fraud, and I could make me five thousand, ten thousand dollars. Why should I go deal with drugs, burglarize someone, you know, rob somebody?" Danny, who purchased gift cards from department stores with stolen identities, described his strategy:

> I get a three-thousand-dollar card. I sell that card for anywhere from fifteen hundred to two thousand cash. See what I'm saying? I got a lot of people that wanted the cards. . . . I made a lot of money doing whatever I do, 'cause that's the type of person I am. Whatever I do, I'm going to be trying to make some type of money at it. If it's not going to make any money for me, I'm not going to do it. It's just that simple.

Of course, those who were involved in mortgage fraud claimed to have made much greater sums than those who cashed fraudulent checks. Some of the offenders we interviewed were mortgage brokers who used stolen identities to apply for loans on homes whose values had been inflated by crooked appraisers. They would then pay a "straw" borrower to receive the loan. Homes that might have been worth $150,000, for example, were appraised for $400,000, yielding profits of hundreds of thousands of dollars.

We cannot say with certainty that the figures provided by participants are precise, as such claims are subject to faulty memories and intentional exaggerations. Nevertheless, the amounts reported by individual participants were consistent across multiple interviews, and comparable with estimates from previous research.[2] Even if we account for potential exaggeration, it appears that most offenders brought in incomes greater than they could have earned from the types of legitimate work for which they were qualified.

Practical Motivations

Previous reports on identity theft have pointed out that some of these crimes are precipitated by the desire to hide from the law or to obtain utilities or phone service.[3] Only three people with whom we spoke mentioned such reasons; all were female.[4] Jolyn told us that because she was subject to an arrest warrant, she used another's identity to get a telephone. While her identity theft started as a means to get phone service, she eventually used this information to garner social security benefits. Jamie said, "I needed my utilities on. [I did it] for that reason. I've never used it as far as applying for a credit card though because I knew that was a no." Sylvia used the identities of others for utilities, housing, and automobiles. In her words, "I just didn't like to have nothing in my name. I didn't like nothing in my name because I was under probation so my probation officer couldn't come in and just check the whole house. He had to just check my room specifically. . . . I never wanted anything in my name because I was supervised release and they can check anything of yours."

How They Spent the Money

Knowing what offenders do with the stolen money is important for understanding why people commit crime and what can be done to control it. For example, if thieves spent the proceeds of their thefts on food for themselves or their families, this would likely elicit a different social (and moral) response than if they spent the money on more hedonistic pursuits. Recent ethnographic research on offenders of various types suggests that the decision to engage in crime is constrained by the social, physical, and situational contexts in which the offender is surrounded.[5] In other words, the decision to engage in crime might seem rational when one's life is riddled with stress, drug use, and excessive partying. It is clear that one's chosen lifestyle is instrumental in determining whether the rewards of crime are worth the emotional, social, and legal risks.[6]

The identity thieves we spoke with varied in the lifestyles they maintained and in how they spent their stolen money. Slightly less than half led self-indulgent lifestyles, characterized by the mentality of "desperate partying" common among persistent street thieves.[7] For these offenders, the proceeds of illicit activities were seldom saved for long-term plans or to pay bills. As Sylvia reported, identity theft was a way of "getting money and getting high." Lawrence described this cash-intensive, drug-infused lifestyle: "I made a lot of money and lost a lot of money. It comes in and you throw it out [on] partying and females. I gave a lot of money away. I bought a lot of things. . . . I mean it's a party." The ease with which money could be made and spent was also reflected in the words of Carlos. When asked how long the money gained from his crimes lasted, he answered, "We were spending it pretty much as fast as we can get it, you know?"

Ed explained what his life was like during the height of his crimes:

> Well at first you're on top of the world because you know you have the best vehicle. I had the best vehicle. I had the best motorcycle. So when I go to the club I go out and come back with three or four chicks. But I knew what it was about. It was about the money, the vehicles, the house, the club, buying dope, and stuff like that.

For these offenders, money was not something to be guarded or saved; it was to be spent immediately and frivolously. In this respect they mirrored the lifestyles of other persistent street thieves, hustlers, and robbers.[8] In fact, those in this group saw identity theft as simply another of their many hustles.

Many who led this lifestyle of desperate partying were addicted to alcohol or other drugs. Sheila reflected the general recollections of these offenders when she claimed that she "was high all the time." Their addictions led them to devote an increasing amount of time and energy toward coming up with cash to fund their habits. For identity thieves, as for other offenders, the inability to draw on legitimate resources eventually precipitated a crisis that they thought could only be relieved through crime. Penny explained her process of getting involved in identity theft, "I started smoking meth, then I stopped working, and then I started doing this for money." Heidi claimed that her drug relapse precipitated her crimes. In her words, "I was clean for three and a half years before I relapsed on methamphetamines and that's what brought me back into [identity theft]."

With the effects of drug withdrawal either present or impending, the risks associated with identity theft were attenuated and the financial rewards accentuated. Gladys claimed that drug use did not instigate her crimes, but it did contribute to her continued criminal participation. "The reason why I say that is because at one time I was clean and I don't think I initially started off for that reason, but after a while it became the reason to continue." Drug addiction, coupled with the inability (or lack of desire) to maintain steady, conventional employment fostered a self-defined dependence on crime. The money made from identity theft was spent quickly on drugs and partying, which then fueled the need and desire for more money. Neal Shover describes the process this way: "Confronted by crisis and preoccupied increasingly with relieving immediate distress, the offender may experience and define himself as propelled by forces beyond his control."[9]

Ethnographic research on persistent street thieves consistently details this criminal lifestyle; however, such behavior was not uniform among our sample. Nearly half of those we interviewed claimed middle-class backgrounds and used identity theft to support lifestyles of the affluent.[10] For the most part, those in this category used the proceeds of identity theft to finance comfortable middle-class lives, including paying rent or mortgages, buying expensive vehicles, and splurging on the latest technological gadgets. In a sense, they were simply trying to "keep up with the Joneses." They did not experience true financial deprivation like those embedded in street life; they simply desired objects that were beyond their financial means.[11] When asked what he did with the money, Jake, a middle-class fraudster, answered, "Nothing more than living off it, putting it away, saving it. Nothing flashy. Just living off it." Bruce, who worked alone and hid his crimes from his friends and family, claimed to engage in identity theft "to maintain an upper class lifestyle. To be able to ride in first class, stay in the best hotels, have the best everything." This is not to say that these offenders did not indulge in illegal drugs, because many did, but their spending was more consistent with the typical debt-ridden American suburbanite than with the average street thief. As Bruce explained, "[Identity theft] was usually for the material gains. . . . At the level that I was doing it at, it had really nothing to do with drugs."

However, even those trying to maintain middle-class lifestyles perceived a need for quick cash. Looming financial problems, including increasing debt and fear of lost income, could lead to a sense of urgency. For people experiencing these situations, the everyday business of paying bills and maintaining their quality of life could provoke feelings of desperation.[12] This is how Jolyn described the circumstances that led her to start offending: "I had a mortgage company that went under—my partner embezzled a bunch of money. Certain events happened and you find yourself out there about to be homeless and I knew people that did this, but they never went to jail." As Jolyn's example shows, mounting sources of crisis can come to represent "threats to status-seeking and status-maintaining behavior."[13] In such cases, identity theft appears to offer relief, even if temporary, from financial difficulties. These identity thieves had much in common with those white-collar offenders who claim that their crimes were motivated more by a "fear of falling" than by the desire to get more.[14]

Regardless of whether our interviewees were street-level hustlers or middle-class fraudsters, it was apparent that their lifestyles influenced their subjective assessments of the risks and rewards of crime. Indeed, members of both groups shared the belief that identity theft offered the financial rewards deemed necessary to forestall desperate situations and sustain whatever lifestyle they chose. The decision to engage in identity theft was seen as a rational and reasonable response given their perceived state of desperation.

PHENOMENOLOGICAL REWARDS: POWER AND THRILLS

Identity theft, like other crime, isn't always about the money. The inherent pleasure that comes from risky and dangerous behavior is an attractive lure for many.[15] Eleven interviewees mentioned that they found identity theft "fun" or "exciting." These offenders enjoyed the "adrenaline rush" provided by entering banks and stores and "getting over" on hapless victims. Bruce said that going into stores "was fairly exciting [because] every time I went to a retail establishment and gave them the credit card I didn't know what's going to happen." Kate said, "It's a high. I've always said my favorite sound is when the credit card clears and the receipt is printing out. It's a natural high." In short, identity theft offered excitement as well as money.

Part of the rush of identity theft came from its ability to put a little adventure in ordinary lives. Jolyn claimed that several tragedies in her life constrained her ability to "truly live" and that identity theft provided an opportunity to live on the edge for a while. In her words, "I didn't get much of a life between my husband dying and the kids getting gone. I just took an adventure. That was the whole point. Replace the money because I'm broke and put a little adventure in my life." Similarly, Danny continued with identity theft simply for the thrill: "I like to go out with money. But eventually it got to the point where I didn't need money. I was just doing it for the high. That is basically what it was: the rush of standing there in her face and lying. [Laughter]. That's what it was. I'm being honest. I didn't need the money. I had plenty."

For others, it was not just the act of appropriating money that was exciting. Instead, it was the internal satisfaction that came from emerging the victor in a risky situation. The thrill came from the feeling of competence or mastery over the victims and the situations. Several mentioned that they felt a sense of power from the "intellectual stimulation" of their crimes. When asked to describe the rush he felt from engaging in identity theft, Lawrence replied:

It's money and it's knowing I'm getting over on them. Knowing I can manipulate the things and the person I got going in [the bank].[16] It's everything. I guess you can say it is a little fear, but it's not fear for me, though. It's fear for the person I got going in there. I don't know. It's kind of weird. I don't know how to explain it. But it's the rush. Knowing that I created this thing to manipulate these banks, you know what I'm saying? They're going to pay me for it and I'm going to manipulate this dude out of the money when they cashing those checks.

When asked what she liked about committing identity theft, Kristin echoed Lawrence's use of the word *manipulate*: "That adrenaline of not knowing. I had three options each time that I committed an identity theft. That was going to prison, dying, or coming home. I knew that those were my choices every day and it was just a rush to get out there and see if I could manipulate the system."

There is little doubt that crime comes with certain non-financial attractions.[17] It appears that identity theft is no exception to this statement. While thrill and power are potent attractors, the identity thieves that we interviewed (with the exception of Danny) claimed money and the lifestyle it affords as their primary motivators. None whom we spoke with claimed that thrills alone instigated their decisions to engage in identity theft. Nevertheless, it does appear that some offenders continued to commit their crimes at least partly in pursuit of the excitement.

One of the things that struck us during the course of the interviews was just how intoxicating some offenders found their lives and crimes. The money and emotions generated by the fraudulent use of others' identities were so powerful and enticing that many claimed they became addicted to the lifestyle afforded by their crimes. In fact, many stated they "tossed around" the idea of quitting, but felt compelled to continue. According to Fran,

> It's very addictive. It's addictive. . . . It's just like a drug or any other habits you can pick up. It's very addictive because I got lost in it. . . . I'm separated from my husband because of it. I lost custody of my kids because of it. And it's just like being on drugs. . . . And I think that's part of the reason why I just matured so much since I've been here [in prison], and I think everything happened for a reason and I think that was my reason for getting out when I got out and getting caught up and I had to pull out of it because it was an addiction. It was sickening. I had got to the point where if I didn't go to bed, I didn't care. . . . I got a credit card, I'm getting out of my bed. It didn't matter if I had the kids with me or not. Keep yourself. I'm going.

When asked what was addictive about the crime, Fran continued:

> I think it was the money. How fast it was coming because when I grew up—there was ten of us—my mom did it on her own. She

didn't pin it on my dad or her husband. She did it on her own. I think leaving from that and then I had my kids early. I had my first child at fourteen. I got married at seventeen. So it was like I was moving fast, but I was still stuck in the same place. It wasn't getting no better. I was like my kids are going to have it better than I had it. That was my mind frame to get what I had to get. For real, it got so addictive that I lost track of what was really my focus. It was not on them anymore. It was on me. I didn't care. I self-consciously didn't pay attention that it was hurting them what I was doing. I just felt like since they had a nice house, had all the expensive toys, had all the expensive clothes, that was being a good mom, which now I realize that's nothing. Materialistic things don't make you a parent.

Dustin explained that he originally planned to steal a certain amount and then desist. He explained why this was more difficult than expected: "Once you walk in a bank and you give a bank a piece of paper and they fork over twelve, thirteen hundred dollars, you're hooked, no questions asked. You know what I'm saying. . . . You're hooked. You're hooked. You're just like, 'Man it's this easy? It took me two minutes to walk in here and do this. I want to do it again.' So you do it ten times a day, you know you got thirteen thousand dollars. As long as that bank account has that money in it to cover that check, yeah."

MAKING EXCUSES FOR THE CRIME

The criminal's ability to interpret criminal behavior in a way that minimizes damage to his or her self-concept is essential for the successful and continued commission of the crime. Criminologists have spilled much ink in explaining this process.[18] Wrongdoers can employ several different strategies to make sense of their crimes and try to align their actions with personal and cultural expectations. One of the most well-known theories for explaining this social-psychological process of sanitizing the conscience is the theory of accounts.[19] According to this theory, individuals use verbal accounts (justifications or excuses) when they want to explain improper behavior. Regardless of which type of account people use, the goal is to neutralize the social consequences of an act that has been called into question. In our interviews, identity thieves justified or excused their crimes in ways that made them appear to be good people who made bad decisions, or to be unlike "real" criminals in some way.

When using justifications, the actor admits responsibility for the untoward behavior, but denies its pejorative content. For example, it is not uncommon to hear college students justify their illegal downloading of the latest pop hits by claiming that they would not have bought the music anyway so the artists aren't really losing money.[20] While there are a number of ways that offenders can justify their crimes, identity thieves relied primarily on denial of injury, denial of victim, appeal to higher loyalties, and sad tales.[21]

Denial of Injury

The identity thieves we interviewed frequently denied that their actions caused any "real" harm or injury. This was the most common justification for their actions. Previous research on justifications and neutralizations has considered the denial of injury a singular category. Our findings, however, suggest that it can be divided into numerous subcategories. While each differs slightly from the others, they all center on the idea that the offender's actions did not lead to any "real" losses, financial or otherwise, to "real" individuals. This statement from Fran is typical: "I always thought that just because it was white collar crime it didn't hurt nobody." Similarly, Joel maintained, "Everything that I did was based on grabbing the identity and then opening separate accounts. It affected them [the victims], but it was different."

Many of the offenders were secure in their beliefs that having one's identity stolen was only a minor hassle and that no real harm came to victims because, with a few telephone calls, any credit damage could be repaired or any financial loss recouped. This justification was most often presented by those who fraudulently obtained and used credit cards. When saying that his crimes didn't hurt anybody, Dustin argued that:

> With credit cards if you notify them that your credit cards were missing then [victims are] not liable. The same thing with forgeries and the bank. If you notify the bank . . . the consumer is not liable. The bank is gonna be insured, so the bank is gonna get their money back. The consumer is not gonna be hurt. Nobody really loses but the insurance companies. It's not taking from an individual per se, like a burglary.

When asked why he did not feel bad about his crimes, Bruce replied, "Well, it's plastic. . . . No one was being hurt. You didn't confront anybody in a negative way, usually. I had to get snotty with a clerk and that's about it. . . . There was never anything bad that really happened." He even went so far as to claim that his indiscretions may have actually helped his victims by bolstering their credit scores. In his words,

> I convinced myself [that] I wasn't going to do anything bad to their credit or to them. It actually may have helped them. I would've gotten them a nice credit card with a high line of credit and it's going to help their credit and stuff like that and then I would close it. It didn't work out that way of course, but at the time I was doing it I didn't think I was doing anything wrong.

Even when thieves stole directly from individuals' bank accounts, they claimed that their victims did not really suffer loss. Despite knowing that the money she was stealing came from someone's savings account, Kendra maintained a guilt-free conscience by claiming the bank would give the money back. "We took all her money out because in our mentality it's like, the bank is insured, regardless," she said. "People are going to get their money back, so nobody's really losing but the bank."[22]

Others denied injury by minimizing the amount by which they actually profited. These individuals contrasted their small gains with those of "real" identity thieves. Ellen claimed, "I mean the money didn't matter to me. It was just [my codefendants] asked me to do it and I just did it for them. It was pocket change. I mean it was nothing."[23] Kenneth was direct in his denial of profiting from the offense: "I never made a dime off any of this. That's why I didn't get much time and I'm here at a minimum security camp.

I never profited from this one iota." Interestingly, even those who made substantial profits tried to minimize their take. In justifying her crime, Sherry stated, "I had the potential to steal hundreds of thousands of dollars—I stole seven thousand. That's all I needed." Despite stealing more than a quarter of the annual salary of an average mortgage closer, Jake argued, "I was making about a couple thousand a week, not really a lot of money. . . . I didn't buy any properties. And I didn't really make that much money."

Others coupled the claim of earning little to no profit with the claim that those who condemned them were crooked and corrupt.[24] Here offenders shifted focus onto the motivations or behaviors of the people who disapproved of them, instead of on their own actions. In these cases they argued that the amounts listed on indictments and reported in news coverage of their crimes were greatly exaggerated by the government, either to ensure prosecution or to make the case sound sexier. As Oscar explained, "You see like in this case, if you ask the government to explain how they got this figure, this amount, they can't explain it." Bradley relayed a similar story: "[The feds] blew up the price of the stuff they had seized to make the points go up so I would get jail time. Because if it would have been below twenty thousand then I probably [would have] ended up getting probation for only like six months."

Finally, seven offenders offered the excuse that they were merely "borrowing" the money. Nearly all of these individuals knew their victims (either casually or intimately) and convinced themselves that they would rectify the situation when they were financially secure. As recounted in his biography in chapter 1, Bruce's theft of a friend's personal information strayed from his usual approach to the crime.

> Sonny was a friend of mine and I was in a bind at that time. I wasn't going to steal his identity of course, I was just going to use his identity to filter some of my clean cash into a fund at that time and then I was going to take it out and go on about my business. . . . I was going to borrow [his identity] for a little while and then get the corporation going. He's going to benefit, I'm going to benefit. I'm going to get a perfect identity and then live from there.[25]

Using a similar justification, Sheila claimed that she did not feel bad about her crimes at the time because she "needed the money as bad as these people did and besides they had it sitting in their account for so long earning interest." She continued, "I'm just gonna borrow it for a minute and [I'm] gonna pay you back. I just can't do it right now so. . . . I didn't think it was really bad."

Denial of Victim

Sometimes offenders admit that their actions cause harm but neutralize moral indignation by denying the victim. In other words, they contend that some victims act improperly and thus deserve everything that happens to them. Offenders defined their own actions as a form of rightful retaliation or punishment, thereby claiming that the victim did not deserve victim status. When identity thieves did acknowledge victims, they described them as large, faceless organizations that deserved victimization because of unsavory business practices. In effect, they claimed that corporations and banks should not be given victim status because of their prior actions of preying on individuals. When asked if he felt guilty for his crimes, Danny explained confidently:

> I mean, like real identity theft, man I can't do that. Intentionally screw someone over—it's not right to me. So I couldn't do it. But corporations, banks, police departments, the government? Oh, yeah, let's go get 'em. Because that's the way they treat you, you know what I'm saying. If they done screwed me over, screw them! That's just the way I feel about it. I'm the eye for an eye type person. You poke out my eye, I'm going to poke out both of yours. That's just the type of person I am.[26]

Dustin went so far as to say that bank executives facilitate and encourage fraud because they actually profit from it.

> Say for instance I'm writing checks or forging $250,000 worth of checks from this bank. When the investigators come in, they're going to say, "Well this bank account was hit for $100,000, the max because that's what they insured for. We know that this guy over here did it. Now, let's see. We can get him to pay if he is convicted.

He'll have to pay restitution on this, but Mr. Bank President, you can file a claim through FDIC for twice the amount of what you were hit for." So in other words, the insurance company's going to pay him back and the feds are going to pay the bank back. They's going to come out with a profit anyway because he's going to write it off in taxes. That's the biggest scam in the world. People just don't see it like that. You're saying, "Well, the bank is doing everything they can to protect us." That's wrong. I believe sometimes the bank makes the availability so easy because it's easy. It's too easy. Sometimes I believe they'll let me get away with stuff. I'm serious. I am serious. I don't know, the bank presidents and security people would probably say I'm crazy, but it's the truth.

Several of the thieves claimed that their victims were in on the scheme and, consequently, they should not be seen as real victims. Jessica justified her actions by saying, "She gave me the passwords. She gave me everything so that I could talk to them like I was her. So although she called it identity theft, she was the one that gave me all this information to have her identity to do this for her." Likewise, Ed had no remorse for his crimes because "the people that gave me most of the information that I received from them said that they had no problem with me using their identity, taking their identity." Dustin also claimed that his victim was in on the crime.

> I had basically everything from where his business location was, he gave it to me. It's not like I stole it. . . . He says he didn't give me permission, but the guy's in prison. He's figuring he's going to get hammered because he ain't supposed to do business with nobody that's an ex-con, so he's going to say [he] didn't know. . . . So that's how I got jammed on this.

Denial of the victim also occurs if the victim is absent, unknown, or abstract. In these situations the offender can easily ignore the rights of victims because the victims are not around to stimulate the offender's conscience. When asked if he thought differently about his crimes after his incarceration, Bradley explained: "Oh yeah definitely because back then I rationalized what I was doing. . . . Because I wanted it so I felt like I should just do it . . . because they're a big company, they got millions of dollars, they don't care and I wanted what I wanted when I wanted it." Bradley also pointed to the fact that, since his crimes were committed mostly online, he could ignore the victims: "I don't have to face anybody. I can go on the computer and be whoever and order you know gadgets and electronics stuff and have it sent to the house." Portraying victims as faceless or "plastic" allowed offenders to distance themselves from their crimes with ease.

Appeal to Higher Loyalties

Many identity thieves also sought to make sense of and justify their crimes by pointing out that their actions were done to help other people. These offenders set aside their better judgment because they thought their loyalties to friends and families were more important at the time. When using this account, they typically framed their illegal behaviors as a means to provide support or to better the lives of their nuclear or extended families. Betty explained, "It's like I tell the judge, I regret what I had put my family through, but I don't regret at all what I did because everything that I did was for the safety of my kids. And I don't regret it. As a mother, I think you do whatever needs to [be done] to keep your kids safe." Echoing this sentiment, Abbey claimed, "I did it for my son. I thought if I had money and I was able to live, have a nice place to live, and not have to worry about a car payment, I could just start a new life and that life is for him. . . . I just wanted my son to be happy and loved." Perhaps the person who best articulated this desire to support family was Joel. In his three-year run as an identity thief, Joel stayed on the move and hid his indiscretions (as best he could) from his family: "My objective was to survive out there. It wasn't to cause a lot of damage. I just didn't want to come back to prison. When I went to prison my kids were babies. I figured I needed to spend some time with them. . . . I knew I was going back to prison, I wanted to make sure they at least spent some time with me, that they saw things, they did things, and they went places." He further explained:

So, what do you do? I mean is there anything that you can't buy, I mean, physically, materially that you can't buy with that kind of money? I mean, jewelry, clothes, you go in and you shop and it makes you feel good that you can buy your kids the clothes you know that they want and you go in and my wife is a shopper: she loves shopping at Walmart and QVC. To be able to go out and go into Saks, or wherever it is, and take my kids over to the Hilfiger section and say, "Okay, here, just get what you want." You know, to be able to do that I guess gives you a sense of gratification for what you're doing for them and you don't realize what you're doing to other people.

In addition to helping their families, several suggested that they were motivated by the altruistic desire to help friends or those who were down and out. In discussing why he did not feel bad about his actions, Lawrence referred to himself as "Robin Hood" because he would "take from the rich and give to the poor."[27] In the following passage, he discusses the good that he did with the money:

I mean there are a couple of cases where I have felt bad. Some people, I mean a lot them, I help out. There's a girl that stay in the projects; I met her at the bus station. . . . I met this female, she was taking her kid to daycare. Her old man was a drug dealer. He wasn't doing nothing for her. She wanted me to drop her kid off at her mom's house, so I dropped the kid off at her mom's and took her back to her house. I went in her apartment. Man, she didn't have anything in there. Nothing. No furniture, no TV. She was drinking out of glass jars and stuff. I'm talking about poor. I'm talking about poverty to the lowest. I felt sorry for her. I ran into the bank a couple of times. She made some money and I let her keep the money. Last time I seen her, she had a car. She had moved up into better place. . . . I just didn't do everybody wrong.

Kenneth claimed that he used his computer expertise to help battered women get new identities and escape their abusers.

I had done some work, back years ago with a friend of mine who happened to be a Catholic priest. He ran battered women shelters around New York City. He had some women that he ran into that were married to psychopaths, sociopaths, kind of sleeping with the enemy concept. . . . [He was] helping them. These women just have nowhere to go. After they broke the cycle of the battered women's syndrome, the going back to the guy and such as that, they were like "this guy is never gonna let me go. If he can't have me nobody can. What do I do?" So like, you gotta do something.

He argued that, since his thefts were not done for selfish reasons, he should not be classified like other identity thieves, who he imagined committed their crimes solely for profit.

Finally, several women who worked at their state department of motor vehicles said they facilitated identity thefts simply because they wanted to help others get official identification. As Daphne explained:

> I helped people that needed an ID. There were some people from Mexico, who I thought were from Florida. There were some just people that had lost their ID over time and were scared to come to the Department of Licensing because they thought they would be arrested, so they asked me to find out what they needed to do to get their license back. . . . I truly thought I was helping people. . . . It was a bunch of stuff on TV about young kids getting shot and they ran because they didn't have any ID and the police were shooting them for whatever, because they ran. And they ran because they didn't have any license, so I caught myself helping them by saying, "Hey, you don't have to go through all that. This is what you need to do. . . . No, you're not going to get arrested if you come in and ask us what do you need." And then it just got to be that people started lying to me, just getting over on me because I was being nice.[28]

By using this account, identity thieves neutralized both internal and external controls, claiming that their behaviors were consistent with their moral obligations to a specific group, usually their families. They did not claim to reject the norms they had violated, as many experienced mental turmoil about their crimes. Instead, they perceived the needs of their families and friends as taking precedent.

Sad Tales

Offering a sad tale was another justification that thieves used to explain their illegal actions. We heard many of these sad tales during the interviews. In such accounts, selected facts about a dismal past were used to explain the state they were in when they committed the offense.[29] Often these tales suggested that offenders were in a desperate situation, brought on by catastrophes beyond their control, and that their crimes were acts of necessity. Thus, these actions did not reflect their true selves, which they claimed were basically good. By invoking this feeling of exigency, offenders simultaneously pacified their consciences and constructed themselves as people worthy of respect. Oscar's description exemplified this mentality.

> You know, sometimes [life's] not easy. You just kind of have this pressure from everywhere. You know what I'm saying? . . . Nobody ever really want to commit crime. Nobody like to commit crime. I don't know if you understand that. . . . Sometimes difficulties and circumstances make people do stuff. So, yeah, I'm not the type. I mean, not a "crime person" . . . it was just circumstances.

In describing the events that led to her involvement in fraud, Jeannette highlighted the overwhelming pressure she was feeling from an abusive husband, mounting debt, and dependent family members. Jeannette felt as if she had no one to help dig her out of this situation.

JEANNETTE: My parents were totally reliant on me for their transportation and stuff to doctors and I just felt like they were asking too much of me.
HEITH: So you felt a lot of pressure?
JEANNETTE: Right.
HEITH: Was it financial pressure from them also?
JEANNETTE: Financial pressure and just, you know, time pressure.
HEITH: Did you talk to them about that beforehand?
JEANNETTE: No.

HEITH: How come?

JEANNETTE: I just felt that I couldn't talk to them. . . . [My husband] was a wife abuser. He was physically abusing me along with mentally so I was trying to prove to him that I have some worth that I can do this. . . . One time when I had an overdrawn account and I was asking him to help me balance my checkbook he went ballistic. So it was a matter that you couldn't tell him anything. If you were a penny short on your checking account he would just be livid. You know? You can't do this right, it was always I couldn't do it right.

HEITH: So it sounds like it was a very stressful time.

JEANNETTE: Right.

HEITH: Not only because of your husband and daughter but the credit cards and that really . . .

JEANNETTE: Right, and my parents were dependent upon me for everything, for transportation and medical needs and stuff like that, so there was like a lot of time constraints and that contributed a lot to my marriage disintegration. I had to be there for my parents so I wasn't there for my husband so it was like a major balancing act.

Sad tales focused on immediate situational pressures and were often coupled with appeals to higher loyalties. In other words, an offender's sense of desperation was often linked with a desire to prevent loved ones from experiencing loss or pain. Interestingly, males and females revealed some differences in the way they articulated the specifics of the tales. Women most often emphasized the abusive habits of men in their stories. Men typically emphasized their desire to protect their loved ones.[30]

Excuses

When using excuses, the actor acknowledges that the act was morally wrong, but denies being fully responsible for it. Excuses are "socially approved vocabularies for mitigating or relieving responsibility when conduct is questioned."[31] For example, consider the situation in which a customer in a checkout line is not charged for merchandise, yet fails to bring it to the attention of the cashier. After returning home, the customer might offer the excuse that she doesn't have the time to go back to the store and wait in line to correct someone else's mistake. In our interviews, identity thieves relied primarily on three forms of excuses: defeasibility, diffusion of responsibility, and scapegoating.

Defeasibility

When using appeals to defeasibility as an excuse, offenders deny willfully taking part in the illicit activity. Actors claim that if they had full knowledge of the situation and motives of others, they would not have gone along with the crime.[32] Though everyone with whom we spoke was convicted of an identity-theft-related crime, not all admitted that they were fully at fault or had done anything wrong. Several who denied their criminal intent claimed that they were conned into committing the fraud or that the authorities greatly misunderstood and misrepresented their actions.

Those who claimed that they were duped into committing illegal activities typically acknowledged that what they were doing was not legitimate but also were steadfast in their claims that they would not willingly engage in illegal behavior. Bonnie was adamant that "we committed a crime but also we were conned at the same time." She further explained:

> You always think you're smart enough not to be conned and I thought I was smart enough. So I don't know if you want to say it, I guess anybody can be conned basically. And when I think about it the people that conned me had never held a regular job. They've been out conning people for thirty years, so they're experts at it. . . . I think that's how the brokers really got me, they seen I was a single mother, with a son, struggling. So they was like, "Oh you don't have to struggle with your son, you can do this." That's basically how it started. And I just always seen myself as someone smarter than that.

Jake claimed that he was unaware of the illegal nature of the transactions he engaged in with his employer until after the fact. As he described the situation:

I started running short on money. [My employer] said, "Well, I got some stuff you can do for me." So I started working for her. In the beginning, it really wasn't like hey, you just jumped into a mortgage fraud scheme. It wasn't anything like that. So I kind of worked my way into it and once I started doing some of her paper work and some of her other stuff, then I started recognizing that this stuff is fraudulent. But I didn't do the right thing and get out of there and leave this group alone. I stuck with it.

Both of these offenders claimed that this type of illegal behavior was out of character for them. They claimed that if they had been a better judge of other people, in a better economic situation, and more in tune with the bad intentions of others, then they never would have participated in the crimes.

Others denied their criminal intent by claiming that partners pinned the crimes on them and that the government forced them to take a plea, despite their minimal participation. Dustin, who pled guilty to his charges, argued, "I don't really think that I'm guilty of identity theft. I think that I'm guilty of accessory or conspiracy, but the way the government sees it, they put so much pressure on you to cop [a plea]." Connie claimed that, since she was the supervisor at the department of motor vehicles, she was blamed for all the actions of the "real" fraudster. In her words, "I thought at first, okay, I'm going to plead guilty because I can't deny my signature is there. I can't deny that, but how am I supposed to know everything? You're in the back and they come to you bringing you the documents or the application and you just go ahead and sign."

Diffusion of Responsibility

Individuals who worked with others to carry out their crimes relied on the diffusion of responsibility to excuse their actions. Although large amounts of money were frequently appropriated, many of the self-proclaimed low-level organizational members in our sample claimed that they played only a minimal role. In cases involving mortgage fraud, for example, the occupational status of participants ranged from administrative assistant to attorney. Although the entire scheme might have netted millions of dollars, an administrative assistant who knowingly notarized fraudulent documents likely earned a "bonus" of a few hundred dollars, while the closing attorneys and mortgage brokers gained hundreds of thousands of dollars.

By comparing themselves to others in the scheme, low-level employees argued that they should not be judged like other "real" thieves. These individuals pointed to the small amount of money they made as evidence that they "really didn't do anything." Jake, who was involved with a team that committed numerous mortgage frauds, minimized his participation in the crimes throughout our interview. In response to a question about punishment, he said:

> I really thought that the punishment would not be as severe as it was only because I didn't really participate directly in going out, searching for people. My role primarily was a paperwork pusher. I would review paperwork. I would help set closings up. I wouldn't say it was a minor role, but it wasn't a role that made the organization go. I'm like well, if I get caught, maybe I can plea out to a month or year or so.

Lois described the following rationalization:

> I never believed that I would be listed on the indictment. . . . I didn't go into it saying okay, I'm going to make a ton of money off of this, you know. . . . When I saw the indictments and some of the amounts of the money that these folks were making, I mean $1.2 million. And I'm a struggling just-out-of-school student. I lived in an apartment that was barely big enough for me. My car was still owned by Mazda, you know what I mean?

While working at a billing agency, Jarred gave lists of customer's names to a fellow employee, who in turn passed the information to a friend. He employed a similar excuse: "I'm an outside guy. I'm not really involved. I don't know what's going on. I'm not making no transactions. None of this money is coming into any of my bank accounts. So I don't have nothing to do with it." Those who occupied "small" roles in street-level networks also were able to diffuse or minimize their culpability for the crimes. Those members who facilitated the creation of fraudulent identification documents (mostly, those working in state department of motor vehicle offices) framed their participation as far removed from the dirty business of stealing money.

Scapegoating

Scapegoating is the allegation that one's indiscretions are a response to the behavior of others.[33] When identity thieves used this excuse, they often pointed to the pressure they felt from co-offenders or those they were indebted to, then directed the blame for their crimes onto these people. Anne claimed, "I've always been a good person. I just got with the wrong person, wrong people, got me in trouble." Emma claimed that she did not want to continue exploiting others' identities but was physically coerced into doing so by her boyfriend. According to her, "Well, he hit me. He didn't beat me up, but I did have bruises. There was physical violence in making me do these things, making me go in these places. . . . It's hard because I have free will and I know what I did. I know what I was doing and I knew that it was wrong, but I did do it. But he did make me." Betty told a similar story of physical coercion from a male, this time an alleged member of the Salvadoran gang Mara Salvatrucha (MS-13).

> I got involved with a guy. He was from El Salvador and he started bringing people into the United States and those people had left the kids behind. When I found out [about his crimes], it was too late because he threatened me. He say if you tell, I will kill you and your kids. So I didn't have no other choice. And he belonged to the MS-13 gang. And all the people from the MS-13 gangs were involved in it.

Several offenders used drugs as their scapegoat. These individuals claimed that their drug use was responsible for their involvement in crime. According to Dale, "I just started experimenting with crack and that's probably what got me back in here this time. . . . I'm never a person that wanted to be rich, 'cause I don't have no kids, I don't have a woman myself to take care of. So, having big money was not an issue to me until I started messin' with drugs." Heidi, who was arrested for passing a fraudulent check to buy a cup of coffee, said:

> When I got busted at that Maverick for the dollar-fifty coffee, I felt relieved, because I couldn't stop getting high. I was a junkie. I couldn't stop getting high until I was locked up and I'd dry out. They keep locking me up for ninety days and then what? I'd get out and go get high again. That's what happens when you're a meth addict and you're a needle user. You can't, you can't stop unless you get help. When you're an addict, you're an addict. You can't stop unless you go and get help.

DENYING THE CRIMINAL IDENTITY

Media reports that focus on identity theft have a tendency to demonize the culprits. It is not uncommon for the media to portray identity thieves either as sophisticated hackers who can capture valuable information as citizens transact their daily business, or as desperate drug addicts who dig through garbage and search mailboxes to find identifying information. The implication of these portrayals is that those who steal identities are ubiquitous predators, willing to exploit the simplest of our routine actions.

The identity thieves we interviewed were aware of the image put forth by media and law enforcement. Their awareness of that stigma likely affected the ways that they presented themselves when questioned about their wrongdoings, and also the ways in which they discussed their motives with us. Certainly, the justifications and excuses that participants offered were geared to present their actions in a positive, or at least understandable, light.

We could take at face value their claims about what motivated them to engage in crime; however, doing so would ignore the assertion that "the differing reasons men give for their actions are not themselves without reasons."[34] In other words, the ways in which offenders describe their motives are designed to present a desired identity to others. This should not be taken to mean that money or excitement isn't instrumental in instigating their crimes.

Looking deeper, however, we can see that, by framing their crimes as a means to overcome self-defined desperate situations or to support chosen lifestyles, offenders can show they are not immoral or irrational actors. If we would simply consider these situational demands, they seem to ask, we would understand that they are practical people who made decisions that were reasonable, if not rational. Similarly, offenders' justifications and excuses are even easier to interpret if we think of them as the means by which offenders portray themselves in a positive light. When they reveal sad tales about succumbing to external pressures and committing fraud, they are painting their actions as out of character, but still consistent with the expectations of the middle class. In the same fashion, an appeal to higher loyalties frames their actions as reasonable for people such as themselves.[35]

When discussing their crimes with us, participants attempted to distance themselves from "real" criminals, a common strategy among white-collar offenders.[36] Regardless of gender, lifestyle, or any other demographic characteristic, the identity thieves we interviewed typically framed their actions and themselves as different from other criminals, even from others who used stolen identities. Some said they switched to identity theft because it was not as morally offensive as other forms of crime, especially those that involved direct contact with victims. For example, Penny found identity theft easier (practically and morally) than other illicit means of making money. In her words: "I know a lot of girls sleep with men for money and I don't do that. Not that I'm justifying what I did, but this was so easy. It was easy money. . . . I don't like to hurt nobody. I don't. . . . A lot of people will jack people. I didn't jack people."

Nearly all agreed that physically hurting someone for money was beyond their capacity, as that was perceived to be morally wrong. Tameka claimed that she and her partner did not commit robberies, because "[we] felt that if you robbed a bank or if you sold drugs or something else, that was beneath us. We didn't do that because we had finesse, we were able to walk in a bank, get money and live." As Christine described, "A lot of people that use meth, I mean like, they'll rob you. . . . I'm not like that. I found an easier way I could [get money] . . . that didn't seem dirty." Similarly, Chelsea explained, "Like I can't see me in all black and busting in somebody's house or robbing a bank. I just can't. I don't know. I don't see it. I'm not a mean person. . . . I'm, I don't know, I'm a kind person I guess." It was apparent that many identity thieves viewed themselves as morally superior to those who engaged in direct predatory crimes, who sold their bodies for money, or who physically harmed their victims. As such, they claimed that they should not be seen or judged like "real" criminals. In short, the ways in which they discussed their crimes allowed them to present themselves as not all that different from the rest of us, preserving a positive self-concept.

|||||||| 3 ||||||||

HOW THEY DO IT

Decades of interviewing offenders—in interrogation rooms, jail cells, and on the streets—have taught us that the criminally inclined are adept at recognizing and exploiting criminal opportunities. This ability to see and exploit an opportunity is typically developed through experience or tutelage from others.[1] Although it is possible to be successful at crime with few or no criminal associates, having such contacts certainly helps. Scholars have articulated how criminals of various sorts organize to share information about criminal opportunities, find places to sell or trade stolen goods, and develop strategies for evading detection or prosecution.[2] By interacting with like-minded others, offenders learn the skills to be successful, the codes of conduct for interacting with other criminals, and a shared understanding of their actions—in other words, a common set of beliefs, goals, and values that approve of and justify involvement in crime.[3]

While it may seem obvious that criminal networks are important for entering and sustaining a career in crime, research on criminal behaviors has not always supported this claim. For example, research shows that those who commit check forgery and embezzlement are able to transfer their legitimate business experiences to a life of crime. In fact, they can become quite successful, despite working alone, without the help of a criminal network or tutoring from other criminals.[4] Check forgers and embezzlers, however, typically are unlike street offenders (such as robbers, burglars, and drug dealers), who require direct contact with victims or the assistance of others to be successful. Whereas street offenders may need partners to serve as lookouts, to provide information on suitable targets, or to dispose of stolen goods, forgers and embezzlers often do not need such allies.[5] Thus, whether one works alone or with others is dictated by the type of crime as well as an offender's life circumstances, such as employment status, proximity to others engaged in criminal activity, and personal preferences (some people simply prefer to work alone).

As shown in previous chapters, the identity thieves we spoke with came to crime along a variety of paths and for a variety of reasons. Some were criminal novices, while others were persistent thieves and hustlers. Most had a history of prior arrest, for offenses including fraud, property crimes, and drug possession or sales. Some hailed from the middle class, while others were raised among the working poor. It stands to reason then that the variations in experience and criminal background among these individuals would lead to different patterns of organization to accomplish their thefts. Our interviews revealed that identity thieves relied on three primary organizational schemes to carry out their crimes: loners, street-level identity theft (SLIT) rings,[6] and occupational teams. Those in each scheme found different ways of solving the problems of locating the personal information of victims and converting it into cash or goods. Each scheme had its own path of initiation, and each came with its own benefits and pitfalls.

WORKING ALONE

Twenty-four percent of the offenders in our sample were typed as loners. These individuals had the least sophisticated form of organization and committed their crimes almost exclusively without the aid of others. Loners typically used the personal information of others to open up credit card accounts or secure bank loans. Many of these offenders claimed that they tried to make payments on the accounts to prevent the victims from discovering the fraud, but mounting debts eventually made repayment impossible. Two loners claimed their victims willingly gave them the necessary information; however, the offenders also admitted to using it in ways not permitted by the victims.

The female loners stole identifying information through their place of work or from friends and family members (both living and deceased). Obtaining information from those closest to them appears to be common among identity thieves.[7] Data from police reports suggests that anywhere from 40 to 60 percent of victims had their information stolen by friends or family.[8] According to victim surveys, in cases where the perpetrator was known, 32 percent of identity thefts were committed by a family member or relative, and 18 percent by a friend, neighbor, or in-home employee.[9]

Marta, a married mother of three who worked at a mortgage company, faced mounting financial problems brought on by chronic gambling. In an effort to fund her growing habit and to hide her financial losses from her husband, she used client information to obtain fraudulent personal loans from banks. Jeannette also faced financial pressures, along with the stress of caring for her elderly parents. She used the personal information of deceased family members to open bank accounts, get credit cards, and apply for a loan from the Department of Housing and Urban Development (HUD). Brandie, a forty-nine-year-old mother of two college students, used a similar method. After the death of her husband from cancer, Brandie began to feel increasingly desperate over unpaid medical bills and the needs of her two daughters. Using the personal information of her children and mother, Brandie took out several bank loans to supplement her income.

Male loners revealed a greater variety of acquisition techniques than did female loners. Whereas women relied on getting information from people they already knew, men were more likely to devise elaborate schemes to dupe people into revealing their information. Joel, whose story was profiled in chapter 1, created fake employment sites across the United States and used the information gathered from job applicants to open business accounts. The scam was quite lucrative, yielding enough money for daily living expenses, shopping sprees, and trips to vacation hotspots. Keith also used a rather elaborate scheme to steal the personally identifying information of his victims.[10] Having worked at his father's medical supply company for a number of years, he had excellent knowledge of the Medicare and Medicaid systems. He would scan newspaper obituaries for information on deceased doctors, then

use that information to retrieve death certificates from the Social Security Administration's Web site. Keith claimed that death
certificates were easy to access as they were considered public information at the time he was committing his crimes. Gathering
information such as names, birth dates, addresses, social security
numbers, and doctors' provider numbers, he would bill Medicare
for services for "patients"—other deceased persons, selected from
newspaper articles and obituaries, whose information he was able
to access using the same methods.

Bruce, who we also profiled in chapter 1, was one of the more
prolific identity thieves in our sample, and one of the few loners
who maintained both an extended period of criminal activity and
a relatively conventional upper-middle-class life. He also exhibited
the most diverse methods of obtaining and converting information. He began his career in identity theft by getting information
from his place of employment. After graduating from high school,
Bruce took a job as a credit and collection manager for a furniture
store. Through his position, he had access to customers' names,
social security numbers, addresses and credit card numbers. He
explained how he first began his crimes: "At that time I was with [a
furniture store]. I was going through credit files and credit bureaus
and seeing people apply for credit and understanding how the
credit bureaus work and seeing what lines of credit they got and it
just kind of dawned on me that I would be able to use this information to gain more money than I was making as a clerk." Eventually
he used other techniques such as stealing from mailboxes, buying
information from online sources, and exploiting his friendships. By
the time he was arrested—fifteen years later—he estimated that he
had stolen the information of at least two hundred people. Bruce
used that information for a variety of identity-related crimes, beginning by applying for a driver's license in someone else's name,
then using it to engage in check kiting. Eventually, he progressed to
mortgage fraud, credit card fraud, and bank fraud.

Bruce maintained that he always worked alone, despite the
sophistication, diversity, and longevity of his crimes. Perhaps because of their isolation from other offenders, such an extended ca-

reer is not typical among loners.[11] In our research, the fact of going it alone appears to be a function of both the need to hide financial problems from friends and family and the offender's lack of criminal contacts. Loners claimed to have entered crime as a "defensive response to private troubles."[12] It was not uncommon to hear them tell stories of desperation after being unable to pay the mortgages on their homes or other bills. As financial problems mounted, they sought solutions, both legal and illegal. This description of loners is particularly true of the female identity thieves we interviewed.[13] These women usually cited pressures related to the care of immediate or extended family. For a variety of reasons, none believed they could share these crises with husbands, children, parents, other family members, or friends. Thus, when confronted with what they perceived as an impending "non-shareable"[14] financial crisis, they chose to engage in identity theft as a quick fix—even though they were living otherwise conventional middle-class lives.[15]

Although female and male loners alike were motivated by a self-defined "need" for money, they seemed to differ on exactly why they needed it. Unlike the women, most of the men who committed identity theft on their own were entrenched in a lifestyle characterized by drug use, crime, and general irresponsibility. Men had lengthier and more diverse criminal histories than most female loners. The majority of the male loners had prior arrests (75 percent) and prior convictions (63 percent); half were embedded in lifestyles similar to other street offenders prior to their current incarceration. Whereas five out of the six women were leading conventional lives, only one of the male loners' lifestyles could be described as such. In addition, the men's crimes tended to be more sophisticated than those of the women.

A few other interviewees resembled the female loners in lifestyle and methods, however, they periodically worked with one or two others in loosely organized groups. For example, Anita and her accomplice received their victims' personally identifying information from a friend who was employed at a doctor's office, with access to patients' files. The accomplice then used that information to open credit card accounts. Anita used her share of the proceeds to pay bills and buy material items. Celine admitted to using a fraudulent driver's license with her picture on it to get a cash advance at a casino with a credit card. This crime was facilitated by her husband, who was heavily involved in identity theft.[16] Although Anita, Celine, and others like them did not commit their crimes entirely on their own, neither did they commit them as part of a team or formal organization.

WORKING WITH OTHERS

Formal organizations are distinguished from teams in that they are "deliberately constructed to perform complex operations with considerable efficiency. They are usually much larger than other forms . . . and their operations extend over time and space."[17] In other words, formal organizations are essentially teams, but on a much larger scale. We identified no formal organizations in our sample. However, 70 percent of the identity thieves we interviewed operated in teams characterized by an elaborate division of labor, in which members performed different roles depending on their knowledge and skills. We found considerable diversity among the offenders who committed their thefts as part of a team. To capture these differences, we divided this category into two types: street-level identity theft (SLIT) rings and occupational teams.

Although there is considerable overlap in the characteristics of occupational teams and SLIT rings, they differ noticeably in the methods used to complete their crimes. Because SLIT rings are organized primarily on the street, members also were less likely to know one another previously than members of occupational teams, which were typically organized at a place of business.

Street Level Identity Theft Rings

The majority (57 percent) of identity thieves in our sample were members of SLIT rings. These rings were characterized by an organizational structure that was hierarchical in nature, but less so than the structure of major criminal organizations such as crime syndicates or drug cartels.[18] Members of SLIT rings are thought to "conspire and loosely organize together for the purposes of illegally acquiring and compromising victims' identities. They have the intent and means to impersonate victims in the course of conducting fraudulent financial transactions for purposes of financial gain against various financial and retail institutions."[19] While some members we interviewed had legitimate employment, the primary context in which they accomplished their crimes was "the street." A typical participant had a lengthy criminal history and was actively involved in street life, with a demographic profile more similar to the average street criminal than the average white-collar criminal.

ORGANIZATION OF SLIT RINGS / The thefts committed by SLIT rings typically were more complicated than those committed by loners. These rings required members to fulfill a variety of roles.[20] Some members obtained victims' personally identifying information, some used that information to withdraw money from victims' bank accounts or cash checks at various businesses, and others provided transportation to the target locations. Depending on the size of the organization, members played one role or multiple roles in committing identity thefts.

Each SLIT ring was headed by a *ringleader*, whose primary responsibilities include recruiting members and assigning the work necessary to acquire information and convert it to cash or goods. The first step in identity theft is acquiring a victim's information; this is the job of the *victim identity source*. Some SLIT rings filled this role with an individual employed by a company that possessed legitimate access to names and personally identifying information of company clients. For most SLIT rings in our sample, however, the victim identity source was a street-level criminal—typically engaged in drug sales, robbery, burglary, or other street crimes— who sold information to the ringleader.[21] Working closely with the ringleader is the *runner*, whose role is to impersonate the victim at financial and retail establishments. Some rings also employed the services of a *credit verifier*. This person would cross-reference victims' names and identifiers, via credit databases, to determine credit worthiness. For example, a ringleader might pay an employee of a car dealership to run a credit check and determine a victim's credit score, or hire someone to call a bank to verify a victim's account balance. A SLIT ring also might include a *fence*, who could find buyers for the goods obtained through fraudulent transactions. (This was most common among those groups who bought items from retail establishments.) Because most of the crimes perpetrated by SLIT rings required individuals to identify themselves at stores or banks, it also was vital to have the ability to create counterfeit documents, such as driver's licenses. A person who fills this role is referred to as the *false identity document source*. Finally, the ring would often include a *driver*. This person—usually the ringleader or a person close to the ringleader—would ferry runners from one destination to another as they perpetrated their crimes. As drivers wait for runners to complete their transactions, they serve both as lookouts and a means of escape but, more importantly, they also ensure that runners do not take more than their allotted share of the profits.

The roles identified here are consistent with those documented by others.[22] However, there were certain members of larger SLIT rings who did not fit any of the aforementioned categories. These members often were performing legitimate jobs (albeit with fraudulent documents created with victims' information), as retail clerks, for example, or employees of state departments of motor vehicles. While they played a significant role in the theft, they did not obtain information or generate the required documents, and thus cannot be labeled either as the victim identity source or the false identity document source.

GETTING AND USING INFORMATION / SLIT rings used numerous methods to acquire and convert information, with larger rings using a greater number of methods than smaller rings. The ringleader was typically a street offender whose previous crimes included identity theft, although a history of property and drug crimes was just as likely. Other team members were drafted from these prior associations. Although in some cases the victim identity source was a company employee who had legitimate access to customers' personally identifying information, SLIT rings relied on other methods to acquire information as well. Some thieves targeted residential and commercial mailboxes to steal checkbooks, bank statements, or medical bills. Others relied on burglary or pick-pocketing to locate information. Still others stole information from their places of employment. When asked where she got information, Penny answered, "I would go into an apartment complex that would have the square mailboxes. There would be like sixty in one, because there's like a little community in there. You just pop it open and there's just all kinds of slots there. You just start taking it all out as fast as you can. [We'd go] real late at night or in the early morning, like when people are just about ready to go to work." Although Fran's SLIT ring sometimes targeted commercial dumpsters located outside insurance companies, her victim identity sources also stole from mailboxes in residential neighborhoods. As Fran described their methods, "Basically it would be the higher quality neighborhoods where mailboxes are at the end of the driveway. You don't want to take the chance of being up on anybody's porch that was our target, but it was not limited to just that because even if they lived in the heart of the ghetto if we knew for a fact they were somebody we could use, we were going to go get them. It was just that simple." Lawrence, who paid other people to obtain information for him, claimed, "I had a dude running into the banks and stealing the trashcans."

Some rings obtained information from willing acquaintances, friends, and family members in exchange for a fee. The "victim" would then wait a while before reporting the "theft." Some "victims" initiated contact in the desire for money, while others were persuaded by ring members to go along. Fran, whose SLIT ring included eighteen members, explained how they convinced people to give up their own information:

> People you know or people you don't know and you meet them. Like my brother, he was in this case and we would get him to meet young girls. He's twenty-seven, so we'd get him to meet twenty-one or twenty-two-year-olds. He'd meet them and he'd

talk them into it, and they're ready. Most of them already have
accounts. Most of them were willing to go open an account after
he introduced us to them, and that was a way of us getting [iden-
tities] other than actually having to buy birth certificates from
[someone].

Victim identity sources also included employees of car dealer-
ships, state departments of motor vehicles, delivery services, and
banks. The majority of such employees were connected in some
way to the ringleader or other team members—as family members
or through other persons embedded in street life. For example,
Dustin described how connections on the street led him to a victim identity source employed at a state law enforcement agency:

> I just happen to meet this lady that was a drug user. She smoked
> crack and worked for the state department of law enforcement,
> so that told me that she could be bought. She was very discreet
> with it, but I knew that she had a weakness. Her weakness wasn't
> necessarily the crack; the weakness was the money from my part.
> I couldn't supply her with crack, but I could definitely give her the
> money to buy crack. So I would make her offers that she could not
> refuse. I'd ask her to go into the file for me and pull up some clean
> names for me. I wouldn't tell her what for or whatever, but she
> ain't stupid either.

After obtaining a victim's information, offenders applied for
credit cards in the victims' names, opened new bank accounts
and deposited counterfeit checks, withdrew money from existing
bank accounts, applied for loans, or opened utility or telephone accounts. Because such transactions all require some form of official
identification, the false identity document source played an important role. Although some occupational teams outsourced this
job, SLIT rings, by the nature of their organization, always handled
it themselves. To produce these documents, teams recruited employees of state or federal agencies with access to social security
cards or birth certificates, which could then be used to order identification cards. While thieves could use fraudulent information to
obtain identification cards through conventional channels, it also
was possible to manufacture false cards using rogue employees of

state departments of motor vehicles, or through street hustlers who had managed to obtain the necessary equipment. (Some offenders specialize in the production of false identification cards for use by underage students to purchase alcohol and by illegal immigrants to apply for jobs.) The SLIT rings led by Fran, Kendra, and Penny all relied on state or federal employees. As Fran reported:

> It was all so easy to get because we had people that worked at different places. . . . My auntie had this lady, a friend of hers that I still don't know to this day, that worked actually in the Social Security Administration. She had boxes of blank birth certificates with the seals on them so I could easily get a birth certificate with your name on it and just take a W-2 form, which is sold in a store. Say I have a small business and I need some forms. I can type up a W-2 form and I have a birth certificate. Go to some driver's license place with just those two pieces of paper and say I need an ID. I lost my ID. It was that easy to get an ID on somebody else.

When asked what kind of computer program her ring used to create fraudulent documents, Kendra answered, "I used the IBM and then Mike's grandma worked at the court system. I don't know what she put in but she put in some kind of bank where it printed it out the same color." Penny described her ring's methods like this: "My friend, he made me the IDs and he was good at it and of course we have a DMV [Department of Motor Vehicles] program from people working at DMV and they get you the program. So we have a DMV program. We even have real DMV holograms, backing, and the paper." Tameka, who served as a runner and second in line to the ringleader, as well as false identity document source, reported, "I had the machine, I had a laptop, every high-tech gadget there was he made sure I had all that. The guy was paid a thousand dollars to show me the software and how to work the machine and stuff."

For SLIT rings, the most common strategy for converting information into cash was by applying for credit cards, both from major card issuers and individual retailers. Offenders could use a stolen identity to order new credit cards, or to issue a duplicate card on an existing account. With these cards in hand, they could buy merchandise for their own personal use, for resale to friends and acquaintances, or to return for cash. Offenders also used the "cash advance" checks that are routinely sent to credit card holders, depositing them in a victim's existing account, then withdrawing cash, or using them to open new accounts.

Among the individual retailers that issue credit cards, Lowe's and Home Depot were popular targets. Offenders preyed on these businesses because of the ease with which they awarded credit. According to Emma: "[I would] go to different department stores or most often it was Lowe's or Home Depot, go in, fill out an application with all the information, and then receive instant credit in the amount from say $1,500 to $7,500. Every store is different. Every individual is different. And then at that time, I would purchase as much of that balance that I could at one time. So if it was $2,500, I would buy $2,500 worth of merchandise." She went on to explain that sometimes she took orders from "customers" before making the fraudulent purchases. Danny explained, "I was buying gift cards and things like that. . . . Gift cards were like money on the streets. People were buying them off me like hotcakes."

Another common strategy for converting information into cash or goods involved producing counterfeit checks. Offenders typically used such checks to open new bank accounts, or deposited them in the victim's existing account before withdrawing cash. Counterfeit checks also could be cashed at grocery stores, or used to purchase merchandise and pay bills. One ring member described the process as follows: "There were some people in my cases that had fake IDs and stuff like that. We use other people's names and stuff to go in [the bank] and cash checks. First they get your account, then they get your name and stuff. Make some IDs and send a person in there to cash checks on your account." Lawrence, the leader of a different ring, explained how he would train runners to cash fraudulent checks:

> Say that the person already got an existing account. I would teach
> the [runner] how to do the signature. I would let him do it couple
> of times, like send him in there and let him practice on it. Then
> once I feel like he got it down pat, I send them in there and let
> them cash checks in that person's name. . . . If the person got an
> account at any kind of bank, you ain't really got to go in there and

cash a check, you can go through the drive-through. So, I send the [runner] through the drive-through with a rented car and just cash the check. But if the person doesn't have an account, what I'm going to do, I'll just take three grand and I'm going to go open up a checking account somewhere. And I just hit the branches around that area. . . . I might get ten pieces in one day, with that three grand in there.

Counterfeit checks were typically produced by the team member employed as the false identity document source, but bank employees also supplied them. In Fran's case, some checks were supplied by the "victims" themselves, then altered to withdraw money from banks:

We went to all the labor-ready companies; they pay people the same day to work. Most of [the companies] give them a check, so what we would do is sit outside of these little companies waiting on these people that just got paid thirty dollars for working all day, offer them one hundred dollars for the check. And we would take the check and duplicate the check. Not the person's name. We tell them you can scratch your name out. We don't want your name. We just need the routing number, the account number, and basically a set up of how the check looks, so it can be duplicated and cashed through different accounts or stores that cash checks. It was just easy to do.

Prior to cashing checks on existing accounts, the credit verifier would ensure that there was enough money in the account. Fran and Penny both took on the additional role of credit verifier in their respective rings. Fran described her ring's methods:

We grew from actually taking money from your account to actually leaving your money in there but using your account to cash bogus checks against. Our thing was to find out how much money you had. If we didn't have the bank statement but we had your account, we just called the bank, "I'm verifying a check and I need to know." We'll type the payroll checks, sit down, make fifteen checks under that one person's name. Cash all fifteen checks in that one day at different branches against that person's account.

According to Penny: "If you gave me a checkbook, the first thing I'm going to do is look at the checks, see where it's from, call that bank, and you can call and do bank verification right away over the phone. So if that check book was good, yeah, it's on. We're going to make an ID for that and we're going to go burn it."

As readers can observe from these descriptions, each SLIT ring did not necessarily rely on a single method to profit from bogus credit cards or counterfeit checks. For some rings, the possibilities even included pre-order and delivery of fraudulently obtained goods. The following dialogue provides a glimpse into one ring's flexibility and resourcefulness.

FRAN: To me that was what we called slow money because you put in an order for a big screen TV. We go get the TV. The TV's fifteen hundred. We charge you six hundred dollars. That was slow money to me because I got to give the person who actually writes the check money, we got to rent a U-Haul to take the truck to get the TV, so that's what we were calling slow money. After a point, I'll say after I was in it five years I learned more about the depositing then.

LYNNE: This merchandise, did you keep it?

FRAN: Actually, it was mostly sold, and for your own personal use if you wanted it for your house or something. But, yeah. Most of the time it was all about the money. If somebody wanted it, we resold the merchandise half price of what it was for. Sometimes under half price because everybody knows it's hot.

HEITH: Would you take orders or would you just go buy stuff and then try to sell it?

FRAN: Mostly take orders so you know exactly what you're going in there to get because as I said, my auntie when she taught me, she taught me don't be unorganized. Don't spend a lot of time in the store. Know what you're going for, get it, and go.

And as Penny's experience proved, neither credit cards nor checks were absolutely necessary for street-level identity thieves to profit from a victim's identity. Numbers alone could be sufficient to enable a fraudulent shopping spree.

They had different hook-ups to where they had more pull, like say over the phone. They had corporate [credit card] numbers and stuff like that. . . . We got a corporate number that we call and if [you have] the person's social . . . it gives you the person's account number and their balance. And all you need to do to shop at [a department store], even if you don't have your plate card, is know the person's social and the right address, or you can add the person to their account, and we do that a lot too. . . . And then you have another thing where you can call this number and you can say I want to put my niece on my account for the day. . . . Give them the social [security number], give them the birth date and the right at-home phone number, and you can go in there and put you on there for the day and go max out your account without no card or nothing. It's too easy.

JOINING A SLIT RING / For offenders who served as ringleaders, recruitment of additional team members was a crucial part of their jobs. They needed people to acquire victims' personally identifying information, verify credit and bank account balances, cash checks, and make false identification documents. Although recruiting could be relatively easy, ringleaders had to tap into a variety of sources (nearly all criminal) to fill their rosters. In some cases, ringleaders purposely targeted particular types of people—such as drug addicts, prostitutes, or other street hustlers—who were thirsty for quick money. In the following passage, Lawrence described how he adapted his recruiting strategy for specific groups.

See once you on the streets you run across prostitutes and stuff like that. Prostitutes have a way of working, doing their thing, and it be going in a person's pocket to get whatever they want to out of a person's pocket. . . . College students is more, you gotta be more thorough with them. They wonder what's going to happen if they get caught and how much money are they going to get out of this. But at the same time, they green. You know what I mean about green? . . . It's like lame or squirrel-like. One thing about college students is they always need money for books, they want to go shopping, you need this, you need that, you need this. As soon as you shoot them with a little dream, say that you can get away with this, it's easy. I'm going to pay you two grand a day. Especially if they can get away with it. The bus station is a recruit too. Missions, all the places like that to recruit people to cash checks.

Ringleaders typically had lengthy criminal histories, which afforded them connections to a large pool of potential "employees." As Penny observed, "there's a lot of tweekers [drug addicts] out there and everybody's trying to make a dollar and always trading something for something." These associations often simplified the recruiting process, with some ringleaders drafting friends and acquaintances with the requisite skills, and others fielding "applications" for positions in the ring. As Lawrence explained, "They just came across something and they knew what I was buying. I mean in any city there's always somebody buying some information." Kendra reported that "people that knew us from the streets, they would come to us, or when they see us, they will approach us. They were asking us because we were high profilers." Fran explained how she recruited people to serve as runners in this conversation:

HEITH: How did you get the people who went into the bank? Did you recruit them, did they approach you, or did you already know them?

FRAN: Half and half. I knew them. They [the prosecutors] say it's twenty-two; I would say I knew eighteen of them, fifteen personally.

HEITH: Did you have to actually talk them into it or was it pretty easy?

FRAN: Everybody was money hungry. You know? Nah, they just seen how I was living and wanted to live nice, just as well.

Accounts of their recruitment by other SLIT ring members generally correspond with the ringleaders' descriptions. Most of the men and women we spoke with were recruited by family members, friends, or acquaintances, some of whom they knew through their earlier participation in street crimes. Regardless of how they were recruited, few required an inordinate amount of convincing (with some exceptions described later in this section). Glen, for example, who sold drugs for five years before turning to identity theft, explained how an acquaintance led him to make the change: "When I was selling drugs, like the lifestyle was kind of getting a little crazy so I didn't want to do that anymore. Then I had met some guy and he was involved in [identity theft] and basically, that's how I started."

Sheila, who became a runner, also described a simple recruitment process. After she and her husband both lost their jobs in the airline industry, she found herself living off credit cards until reaching her credit limit. With a history of drug use, prostitution, and shoplifting, she returned to these crimes. Some time later, she was approached by an acquaintance who asked if she knew anyone who was interested in identity theft. Her decision was swift. As she explained, "I was with [an ex-boyfriend] for twelve years and he showed me how to do it all. So I knew how to do it and I knew if I did it, it was fast money. You know it's fast. If you need money. . . . It's really easy."

Other female offenders in our sample, many of whom had little to no criminal history, were recruited into SLIT rings by family members or intimate partners. Fran, who eventually became the leader of her own ring, described how her aunt taught her the business.

My aunt came to Memphis for my grandfather's funeral and she stayed at our house and she explained to me what she was doing, how she was doing it, and she asked me if I had a bank account and I told her yeah. Me and my husband had a bank account and that was my first time using my own, being introduced. She was like I'm going to put money in your account. You won't get in no trouble. You can clear your name, all you got to do is say that it's not you on the screen. And I'm like okay we can do this. I know we look nothing alike. If she gets in trouble, hey, it's her. But she didn't even do it. I was eighteen and my auntie was like thirty-six or thirty-seven at this time. It was just like she said. Everything went smooth but I gave her my birth certificate and my social security card to get an ID. Well, I don't know what happened because when she got the birth certificate and the social security card, she changed it to meet her age, the birth certificate, and she got an identification with my name, social security number on it, date of birth was changed to a birth date that would fit more to her age group and when I went in, she told me what to say. She told me to say somebody took my purse off the car seat and get a police report and a number and all that. Bank cleared it just like she said it would. They gave me a new account, gave me new checks. They did exactly what she said so now my mind frame is set up to think I can get away with this again. So my second time, I opened up a new account at a totally different bank and did the same thing. This was just routine then, and I was using my own name, and then when she went back and forth between Tennessee and New York and as she came back throughout the years, every time she started something different, she'd bring the idea with her to Tennessee and I'm catching on and I started trying anything and everything that she brought to me.

The women in the sample who were recruited by intimate partners provided the exceptions to these stories of willing consent. In some cases, these women were persuaded by threats of violence. According to the women's reports, boyfriends or husbands often played on a desperate need for money or a sense of loyalty to manipulate them into compliance. In the following passage, Emma explained how she was convinced to participate in another SLIT ring after a stint in state prison for identity theft.

My fiancé and I had a falling out. We split up and I was really upset about that because we'd been together for five years and been through a lot. So fortunately, I ran into this guy that I had known from before, when I was doing [identity theft] with these ladies. He knew that I had done the identity theft and he is a big ringleader and he knew that I was at a vulnerable moment. He knew that I had split up with my man and he approached me on a personal basis and we began an affair. And then he quickly went into okay, well, why don't you do this for me? Why don't you do this? Take this ID. I'll do this and you can run in and you can get some stuff. He knew that I was upset, that I didn't have any money, that I was on DSHS [Department of Social and Health Services], that I was going through some psychological problems. I went ahead and said that I would do that. So I went and did the identity theft.

Betty, who became a false identity document source, told a similar initiation story: "I met him in a restaurant. We became friends and at that time I was a single parent, I was living with my daughter by myself and stuff. And he tell me if you ever need help, if you ever need somebody. I didn't have no car so he say if your daughter gets sick, I can take you to the hospital and stuff like that. And we became really good friends. And then like any other woman— I was lonely—I fell in love with him. It's something that just starts wrapping you around and you don't know what's going on until you're all inside and you cannot get out. There's no returning back." As our conversation continued, she then described how threats of violence and the unsolved murder of her father effectively limited her ability to leave the ring.

BETTY: He said if you tell, I will kill you and your kids. So I didn't have no other choice. And he belonged to the MS-13 gang. And all the people from the MS-13 gangs were involved in it. I want to [stop], but it's like right now, somebody tells you if you stop, your kids will be dead. He say you will never see them. I believed him. My father was the only person that knew what was going on and until this day, I believe he was the one who killed my father. One day he told me the same way you lost your dad, you can lose your children. He never told me [he] did it, but he told me just like that on the phone—I told you, you should have never told nobody and you did tell your father.

LYNNE: Did he ever physically threaten you or just your children?

BETTY: He abused me a couple of times. That was the first time I said I'm not going to do this. I'm not going to. He said this was going to be going on, this is what you're going to be doing, and he left me so bad. My face and everything.

Leaders of SLIT rings were consistent in the observation that plenty of people were willing to jump at the opportunity to make fast and easy money. The statements of many lower-level ring members supported this observation, with little force needed to push them into participation. Some ringleaders recruited members from street hustlers they knew or had worked with previously, while others targeted family members and significant others. Those ringleaders working primarily with other street offenders may have had high turnover, but they also had a ready supply of labor with which to replace departing members. In contrast, those working with family and intimate partners—some of whom had little to no criminal history—often used threats and manipulation to keep them from leaving.

Occupational Teams

Members of occupational teams used their legitimate place of employment to steal information and convert it to goods or cash, acting almost exclusively with fellow employees to commit their crimes. These offenders closely resembled other white-collar fraudsters, such as embezzlers, in that they displayed the outward signs of conventional success. In mortgage fraud schemes, the majority of players were employed at the same company or at companies that worked together to process home loans. In cases involving workers at a state department of motor vehicles, an outside source provided information to employees, who then issued state identification cards or driver's licenses that were subsequently used to carry out identity thefts. As with SLIT rings, occupational team members each had a specific role to play in the crime. However, their crimes typically involved theft on a larger scale, characterized by numerous victims and high dollar losses.

GETTING AND USING INSIDE INFORMATION / Like SLIT rings, occupational teams featured a ringleader, victim identity sources, runners, and credit verifiers. In most cases, all of these roles were filled by in-house personnel. In other cases, the victim identity source might be an employee at another mortgage company or an agency involved in the mortgage process, such as a law firm or brokerage.

In the following conversation, Jake, an attorney, explained how his team was organized and how they acquired information on their victims.

JAKE: Since I was an attorney, they pretty much tried to keep me in that role of doing closings and those types of things. I wouldn't do the closings. I would go with people they would have scheduled for closings. So primarily I was doing whatever little paperwork that there was. The group consisted of about ten people and the lady that I was working with, she was pretty much the center of the group, had been doing real estate fraud for lord knows how long. That was her background. . . . Once I started running short on money, she said, "Well, I got some stuff you can do for me." So I started working for her. In the beginning, it really wasn't like [I] just jumped into a mortgage fraud scheme. It wasn't anything like that. So I kind of worked my way into it and once I started doing some of her paperwork and some of her other stuff, then I started recognizing that this stuff is fraudulent.

HEITH: How would she get the people's names?

JAKE: She had very creative ways. A lot of her stuff was word of mouth. She had a network of brokers that she worked with. A person would come in and apply for a loan and for some reason or another [he or she] wouldn't qualify, whatever the case may be. She'd get a referral from some of her brokers because she had brokers that she dealt with and these guys were in the real estate fraud too. They would give her a referral and say, "We just got this person, got a great Beacon score but for some reason or another doesn't have a job and doesn't qualify for a loan.[23] Maybe you can work with them. Then she would check with them, feel them out, however she did it. If that person seemed like they were interested in purchasing a house, she'd work with them, but most of the time the people she dealt with was either word of mouth or reference from somebody she dealt with.

One of the more elaborate mortgage fraud schemes described by our participants involved employees of several companies and a large state university. The victim identity source was a university student who supplied the personally identifying information of other students. As a university employee, the student had access to records that included victims' names, addresses, birth dates, and social security numbers. He forwarded the information to a real estate broker in a neighboring state who, in turn, used appraisers, underwriters, and a law firm specializing in real estate closings to earn millions of dollars from fraudulent home mortgages. The team included more than twenty-five people. Jolyn described how the team was organized and the role she and others played in the commission of the mortgage frauds.

JOLYN: A lady that I had known was doing some strange and unusual loans. She wanted to get together and do it as a partnership, and I needed the money. As I said I was going under and so the deal was I bring in the people that want to do it, she'll find the properties and make sure we get the value. . . . And that was the deal. And she wanted to handle the money. I figured the calculations sheets and I knew who was getting what, but the people that were involved in our group, the borrower would walk with $25,000 or $15,000 and then Wendy and I sort of split what was left over. I coordinated the appraisals. Made sure that we had appraisers that would do it and found the properties.

HEITH: They would give fake appraisals?

JOLYN: They weren't fake. They were based on real properties that sold at that price, but I knew that those properties had been jacked up. They were real comps but those comps were squirrelly.

LYNNE: So they inflated the value of whatever property that it was?

JOLYN: Yeah.

One of the paralegals on the team, Lois, explained how things got started and the role she played in this large-scale fraud.

LOIS: While I was working with [my co-offender] she started doing real estate closings. And I initially was just doing the general practice portion of it, like car accidents, personal injury things of that sort, while she did the real estate and then she phased out of the real practice and started just doing strictly

real estate and I became her post closer. And I just did nota-
ries, I did the documents that went off to the lender. . . . While
that was going on I was still attempting to study and do other
things. Initially, when she first started doing the closing business, the way it set up, well, what the law says is that when
you're a notary public of course you have to witness the signature when someone signs. But as the business got quicker and
quicker there would be times when I'd be away studying and
there'd be closings and I'd have to witness once I got back.

LYNNE: So when you were notarizing, you didn't actually see a
person's ID?

LOIS: Exactly . . . the IDS were actually in the folder. . . . So, I was
thinking okay, well there's the driver's license, so I'll go ahead
and notarize.

LYNNE: But you didn't see the person.

LOIS: I wasn't present to actually see them 'cause I would, a lot of
times I would, study during the day and take classes during the
day preparing for the bar. And come in the evenings and do
whatever post closings, or whatever they had done during the
day I'd finish it up in the evenings.

JOINING THE TEAM / Depending on their particular knowledge, skills, or relationships with others, an occupational team
member might gather victims' personally identifying information,
create false identification documents, appraise a home, or notarize
closing documents. To begin the fraud, however, the team must
have a leader. A ringleader's job entails convincing others to participate, keeping them motivated and on task, and organizing the
group so that they can be successful. Because occupational teams
are organized in a place of business with a ready supply of potential
team members, this task was often less complicated than it might
have been for the leader of a SLIT ring.

Occupational team ringleaders relied on a number of methods
to convince their employees to participate in criminal activities,
but regardless of their methods the process was relatively easy. For
employees facing financial difficulties or mounting debts, merely

witnessing their bosses' affluent lifestyles was enough to convince them to participate when asked. As with many of those who were part of an occupational team, Abbey took what she perceived to be a legitimate job, only to find out later that her superiors were engaging in mortgage fraud. She explained how the apparent financial success of her boss—the ringleader of an identity theft and mortgage fraud scheme—and his associates influenced her decision to join the team: "[My boss] was doing it and his friends were doing it and anybody who was associated was doing it for years. And that's what made me want to do it. I could see all these people are my age and they're like super successful. They have all those properties."

Ringleaders were adept at using their employees' financial difficulties or desires for easy money to their advantage. Abbey described how her boss also played on her sense of loyalty during the recruitment process.

> The first month, I knew there was something a little weird. And he would just mention his investors and he'd have like a smirk on his face. And I'd be like, Hmm. And then I would start looking through all their files and I'd start looking things up online to see who really owned the properties, and I'd start figuring out and looking at everything. And I said, "You're an investor, aren't you?" And he's like, "I think I can trust you Abbey." He told me everything. He got his business partner and the two of them sat me down and they said we're going to tell you the truth; and do you still want to do this; and they've been doing this for years. So I thought I'll stay and see because I needed the money. I was at a point where he built his loyalty with me because when I decided to leave my husband he paid for me to get my mortgage broker's license. He paid for me to get an apartment, the down payment, and everything. He paid for me to get all brand new furniture for my apartment. So here, that's like loyalty. I did this for you, Abbey, because I know with the couple of closings that I'm just hand feeding you, you're going to pay me back, which I did but it was like the glue that kept me there.

Jake, who also was involved in mortgage fraud, explained how his first steady job led him to the crime. Like Abbey, he took a position in what he perceived as a legitimate business but soon learned that his employers were involved in illegal activities: "Well, what happened to me was after I got out of law school, I pretty much had a hard time finding a job, so I started doing some things for myself. I met up with these people that were doing real estate. . . . I graduated from law school, worked a few jobs here and there. I pretty much didn't get anything stable, so I got with these people that were doing mortgage loans, started working with them. By the time that I figured out what they were doing, I was already involved with the process."

A few offenders in our sample were not struggling financially; for them, the prospect of making more money—and making it quickly—was the attraction. Carlos, who earned over $70,000 per year as a manager for a national drug store chain, talked about how the extravagant lifestyle of his ex-wife and her new husband influenced his choice. When asked how he got involved with these crimes, he replied:

> Basically, I would say greed pretty much. My first wife, or best friend, was named Karen and the guy who really was the mastermind behind this whole scheme named Jack and they were married. . . . She said, "You could make a shitload of money, why don't you just come and do this?" So I took a flight out there, I stayed out there for two weeks taking a training. (They had a course, like a school inside their company that you could go and learn how to do loans.) I think my first month I made about twenty-three grand. Which is, damn, a shitload of money for me considering I was making between seventy and eighty a year working for Walgreens. So, I kind of stuck it out and kept doing it and doing it. Next thing you know I am flying out to Denver more consistently because they're living the lifestyle that really I wanted. They have hundred-thousand-dollar cars in their garage; they're living in a million-dollar house; they have anything they wanted. They went on a vacation three times a month, they're flying in their own jets, they've everything you could think of that you want. That is pretty much it. They had it. And while I was there I was living a different life because I am driving a hundred-thousand-dollar car because I am their guest. I am living in this house and it was great because I knew her my whole life pretty much and her hus-

band was cool as shit, so why not hang out with them [and] do this. So one thing leads to another and I started doing these property deals with them.

As reflected in their own words, the turn toward crime came rather easily for most of the offenders who participated in an occupational team. Their bosses or coworkers (or, in Carlos's case, an ex-spouse) convinced them to join, taught them the necessary skills, and provided the excuses and justifications necessary to overcome any misgivings.

PROMISES AND PITFALLS OF WORKING IN TEAMS

The decision to work alone or with others carried different consequences for the offenders in our sample. Two obvious benefits of working alone are that thieves do not have to split profits with others and they have no codefendants to inform on them. This is certainly not the case for those working with others, particularly for those involved in large groups. As the number of team members increases, the risk of one member getting caught and becoming an informant also is likely to increase. On the other hand, group members have the benefit of their criminal partners' experiences and expertise, while solo offenders have no one who can share labor or provide social support for their illicit endeavors.

The crime's level of sophistication did not appear to affect a loner's reasons for working alone. Some wished to hide their financial problems from friends and family, others simply had a lack of criminal contacts. Identity thieves with longer criminal histories expressed concern that working with others would increase their chances of getting caught by law enforcement. Danny, who used stolen information to open bank accounts and withdraw money, explained why he entered the banks himself rather than hiring others: "When it comes to that type of stuff, I'm not really a people person. I don't trust a lot of people. It's just, because it's so much snitching and stuff like that going on for the past eight to ten years . . . I been like uh-uh. Plus, I been told on two or three times myself, so, that's how I got caught up with the feds in the first place—somebody telling on me." Jay preferred to work alone for similar reasons. When asked how he learned to make fraudulent IDs, he said: "Trial and error. . . . I didn't get taught much . . . I was always trying to find someone that was good. Every time I found someone that was good, they weren't worth a shit anyway. What they said they knew I could figure out in a week and I had to worry about them because that's what always got everyone busted was other people." Joel echoed this opinion: "[I worked] by myself. I couldn't trust anyone else to know. I mean, there were so many people looking for me, I didn't go around anyone else."

In addition to the increased risk of apprehension mentioned by these offenders, participation in a criminal group also may lead to more severe legal penalties for some individuals. Many of the offenders we spoke with claimed that their criminal participation was exaggerated by co-offenders who were attempting to minimize their own roles and subsequent legal penalties. Unlike loners, who remain solely responsible for their participation in identity theft, members of occupational teams and SLIT rings have plenty of others to which they can shift blame.

Despite these drawbacks, however, identity thieves joined occupational teams and SLIT rings for the real advantages they provided in committing crime. In these larger organizations there are more people to acquire resources, to assist with task management, and to devise strategies for avoiding law enforcement agents.[24] For example, many of the identity thieves we interviewed spoke about the need for the specific knowledge and equipment required to make realistic identification documents. Penny's conversation underscores the importance of social connections in the success of the crime:

PENNY: We had [plates for] fifty states . . . They were called, I can't remember the word right now. They were called like a plate, like a hologram. The program for the computer for every state was a license. It had all fifty states.
HEITH: How'd you get that?

PENNY: It came from somebody, who came from somebody, who came from somebody that worked at the DMV. It's a program. . . . I really didn't get on the computer part. Somebody else did.

Another advantage to working as part of a team is that other members often provide the excuse or justification for engaging in crime.[25] In some sense, committing identity theft may be less stressful for those working as a team because of the social support they receive. Other members, typically the ringleader, persuade individuals to join and encourage them to continue as doubts or guilt surface. (Of course, whether this is an "advantage" or not depends on your perspective.) For example, Ed explained how the person who recruited him minimized the moral and legal consequences of the crime: "Basically he said that identity theft was the most overblown conspiracy there is to mankind, there is right now, as far as insurance. And he said, all these people going out, [saying] they lost this and they lost that and blah, blah, blah, but they don't lose a thing. They get a new job and get some paperwork and go get a new identification, whatever, a new driver's license number and they take it and they get their credit erased, but people are already having problems."

Working in a team also can provide offenders with the opportunity to profit from side deals, in addition to their share of the team's earnings. For example, Jolyn, who coordinated the appraisers for the mortgage fraud scheme led by Carol, used her connections with other team members to purchase a social security number and open her own fraudulent bank account. Similarly, while processing fraudulent real estate loans for her boss, Abbey also bought a property for herself. In this case, Abbey used her son's social security number and her own maiden name to purchase a property for investment purposes. Such practices seemed to be more common among members of occupational teams than SLIT rings, although SLIT ring members did express distrust of others in their groups. For example, several SLIT ring members suspected that their victim identity sources were reselling the same information to outsiders, while others suspected their runners of using the bank account or credit card numbers of their victims to commit their own frauds.

As we mentioned earlier, group members can provide social support for others by downplaying both the risks of getting caught and the anticipated legal consequences. While a possible advantage from one perspective, the misperceptions that result proved a decided disadvantage for some of our interviewees. Some thought their risks were lessened by their lower levels of participation, believing that prosecutors would be more likely to target the "big fish" in the scheme. Other offenders imagined that they could easily shift blame to other members of the team. Many of these assumptions were incorrect. In such cases, the persuasive rhetoric of others led to a false sense of security. In a scheme that generated losses of thousands or, in some cases, millions of dollars, each member could be held equally responsible. During prosecution, lower-level members of the team frequently had little information with which to bargain for leniency. As Lois, the paralegal involved in a large-scale mortgage fraud, explained:

> It was such a media frenzy when it happened by it being such a huge fraud case. I think $11.2 million was the final amount of the homes and the damage that was done. And I think just by that time it was really more of a head count. We got so many people so they really just wanted anybody that had any kind of certification. They took all the real estate attorneys that were involved, they got their licenses, they got any attorneys that even touched the case. And I didn't know enough to get myself out of trouble but I was involved enough to stay in the trouble. 'Cause with the government, the more information you can give 'em, the better your deal will end up being. They kept saying come on Lois you gotta tell us something, you gotta tell us something. And I was like I told you everything I know.

Jake, the attorney who was involved in fraudulent mortgage transactions, faced a similar situation: "The overall group was probably responsible for anywhere between five hundred [thousand] to a million dollars worth of damages in mortgage fraud on people.

They gave me restitution of five hundred thousand. What I felt they should have done was say we will divvy up—if the group was responsible for a million, let's figure out and attach each individual for their part in it."

Members of SLIT rings often faced the additional risk of being associated with individuals involved in street crimes. If, for example, the victim identity source also was engaged in drug selling, the risk of detection increased. Furthermore, when such street offenders were arrested for unrelated crimes, they often gave up information on SLIT rings and their members in an effort to minimize their penalties. When asked what led to her arrest, Gladys, whose SLIT ring included drug users and sellers, responded, "People. I was dealing with other people. That's what got me caught. That's where it started from, someone telling."

|||||||| **4** ||||||||

HOW THEY REDUCE RISK

Most persistent offenders give little thought to the possibility of a lengthy prison sentence when in the midst of a crime. Instead, they focus on the potential rewards of the crime and on the technical challenges it poses. The potential for arrest is approached as a problem to be overcome, not something to agonize over or weigh in fine detail.[1] Drug addicts in particular may be willfully inattentive to legal threats, in hopes of minimizing the immediate discomforts of addiction. Some offenders become accustomed to the risks and reconcile themselves to occasional failure, while those who believe they have little to lose are not deterred easily. Other thieves enjoy the adrenaline rush of crime, likening it to the effects of chemical stimulants, fast driving, high-stakes gambling, or fighting. This is particularly common among young offenders, for whom an increased threat of penalties can result in an increased emotional high.

Risks are present at all stages during a criminal event, and perceptions of these risks do affect behavior. But the perception of fear in settings that spawn criminal acts can differ considerably from what is commonplace in more deliberative settings, where clear-headed potential offenders look at crime and its long-term prospects. The deterrence lessons of the penitentiary and the policies contained in complex sentencing tables can seem remote when identity thieves in action weigh the risks and potential rewards of their crimes. In the contexts where street-level thieves choose crime, for example, formal threats and repercussions are pushed to the background of attention, are seen as improbable, or viewed as acceptable contingencies. Effective deterrence at that moment requires that the appropriate message be delivered to potential offenders. The challenge is to imagine and create the circumstances in which fear will work.

Greater emphasis, therefore, must be placed on understanding the risks present during criminal events and the techniques that offenders use to manage these risks. Some researchers have suggested that legal threats assume more importance when offenders have already begun their crimes.[2] The possibility of discovery causes many young auto thieves to cut short their joyriding and many burglars to leave the home even if staying longer could increase profits.[3] Offenders are able to overcome the threat of the law when committing crime, but the possibility of arrest is still recognized at each stage of the criminal event and understandably constrains how offenders behave. Thus, examining the ways that offenders assess and overcome the risks associated with crime is necessary if we are to understand the decision to offend and develop effective ways to curtail this activity.

PERCEPTIONS OF RISK

Ethnographic research with persistent street offenders such as burglars, shoplifters, and robbers indicates that, for the most part, they do not dwell on the potential long-term risks of their enterprises.[4] Identity thieves appear to be no exception. Half of those we interviewed claimed to ignore completely the possibility of formal consequences. While slightly less than half acknowledged that they thought they would eventually be imprisoned, even these offenders did not think they would be caught for this particular crime. Sheila explained, "I looked at it like I'm not gonna get caught today, you know. I'm gonna make it through this one today." When asked if she ever thought about getting caught, Kendra answered, "Yeah, but you know at the time you really don't think about it like that. Everything has consequences. It's just like people out there who sell drugs. For the moment they know they aren't going to get caught, but in the long run they will." Heidi realized that she would eventually get caught because "you don't run forever." When asked why she persisted in crime, despite this knowledge, she struggled to articulate her reasons: "I guess you would say, like, I'm gonna get caught. I'm gonna get caught. I know I'm gonna get caught. I'm gonna do it though because you know I'm stupid. [laughs] I know they're gonna catch me, but I'm gonna still do it kind of thing. I don't know. It's a stupid thing to do and you know that they're cracking down on it, but you still do it. I don't know. The dumbest criminals, have you ever seen those videos?"

Even though many offenders believed they could not continue committing identity theft with impunity, this belief had little deterrent effect. While Heidi had a difficult time identifying her reasons for continuing with crime, others did not, pointing to the fear of experiencing drug withdrawals, for example, or the assumption of lenient penalties. As noted previously, many of the identity thieves we interviewed recognized that they could obtain a great deal of money for their efforts. Thus, when asked why the potential for arrest did not stop him, Carlos replied, "I thought we might get caught, but again the scheme had been perpetuated for so long and nothing had happened. . . . I still thought about the money the whole time." Sylvia reported that her financial troubles took precedence over her concerns about detection.

HEITH: While you were out on the street did you ever think about getting caught?
SYLVIA: Yeah, but I didn't care.
HEITH: Why not?
SYLVIA: Because, I had to keep on living. Fear wasn't going to pay my bills for me.

In assessing the costs and benefits of identity theft, offenders were quick to mention their relatively low expectations of punishment. When asked if she ever thought about getting caught, Fran responded, "I did, but as I said, my mind frame was that it's white-collar crime. At that point in time everyone that was getting [convicted of] white-collar crime was getting a slap on the wrist." Several thought they would simply lose their jobs or, at most, receive probation. In Anne's words, "I didn't think I'd be arrested for just doing two people. . . . Fired from my job? Yeah, that's the worse I thought I'd get." By Jolyn's assessment, the potential punishment would be "not so bad. I knew I might have to go plead [guilty] and I knew I might have probation because back then that's about all you got. A fine and probation and you can never do mortgages again." Lawrence, who was sentenced to three years, stated, "I ain't knew they'd give me this much time. I thought because of a white-collar crime I'd get a slap on the wrist and like probation or something." According to Brandie, "I thought if we got caught we would possibly get—since I hadn't been in trouble before—probation. That's what I thought."

Even those who anticipated incarceration had low estimates of the sentences. Mindi, an immigrant who was sentenced to almost six years, explained:

> I thought I was going to get caught. I did, but I didn't think it was going to be this big. I thought I was going to go to jail for a couple of months or something, not seventy-one months . . . [I thought] I would just pay for it for a little while and get out. Never in a million years I would think that all of them (my family) would be deported and we lose everything, the cars, the houses. Nothing like this ever, ever crossed my mind. Which is stupid because what happens when you walk the crooked line? Somebody's going to pay for it, but I didn't think I was going to get seventy-one months.

Mindi was not alone in this belief. Bridgette thought she'd get "maybe a year or something in a state prison. I never knew. I never knew the extent of it when I was doing what I was doing." Such beliefs about the lenient punishment of white-collar criminals were based primarily on stereotypes about a class of offenders who were more likely to hold higher social status, have otherwise legitimate occupations, and possess the ability to bring great resources to bear on their legal defense. Many of the identify thieves in our sample enjoyed none of these advantages, and failed to realize that their own "illusion of invulnerability" was based on a faulty comparison.[5] They calculated their risk of sanctions by comparing their behaviors to the crimes of well-known figures such as Martha Stewart or Richard Scrushy. Identity thieves who perceived the consequences of their acts in this light severely underestimated their potential punishments. In fact, research on sentencing outcomes shows that the typical white-collar offender (such as an embezzler or fraudster) receives comparable punishments to those who commit street crimes (such as robbery, burglary, or larceny).[6] Considering our interviewees' beliefs that little harm would come to them, coupled with the perceived high financial or intrinsic payoffs of the crime, we can better understand the attractiveness of their choices.

While offenders such as Fran, Jolyn, and Brandie at least considered the possibility of arrest, others devoted almost no thought to this eventuality. This ability to ignore the potential legal consequences of their crimes was exhibited by half of the identity thieves we interviewed. When asked if he ever thought about getting caught, Glen responded, "Not really. I mean, I knew there was always a possibility, but that wasn't really on my mind." Penny replied, "Nope. I didn't care because I was good at what I did and I know I wasn't going to get caught." Similarly, Bradley answered, "Not really. I mean . . . that wasn't really on my mind. At the time I was just worried about getting money."

One reason that Glen, Penny, Bradley, and others like them gave for not dwelling on risks was the perception that such negative thoughts were detrimental to their immediate and long-term success. They were convinced that, by devoting mental energy to the potential pitfalls of their actions, they would unwittingly act in a suspicious manner, attract unwanted attention, or make careless mistakes. To guard against such outcomes, they tried to think positively and maintain an optimistic outlook. This is how Bruce described his mindset when entering banks and stores for illicit purposes: "It's very super-optimistic. I mean you have all the trappings around you of extraordinary success and everybody around you thinks you are extraordinarily successful. I mean you have the look of somebody that is completely in the upper echelon. I just got in that mind where I was not going to get caught."

In describing her experience with crime, Mindi explained, "When you get too comfortable doing illegal things, you become like, it's just like you get a superpower. You don't think you're going to get caught." Like the athlete who visualizes a winning performance or repeats a positive mantra before competition, identity thieves entered the criminal arena thinking only of success. After all, ordinary citizens, confident in their conventionality, typically have no problems making routine transactions, such as cash withdrawals. Identity thieves therefore believed that, by acting like ordinary, confident citizens, they too could withdraw funds without harm to themselves.

Negative thoughts would only make their tasks more difficult by introducing self-doubt and uncertainty. Many claimed that they pushed negative ideas aside by uttering simple phrases, such as "fuck it" or "to hell with it," then forcing themselves to plunge into the criminal event. For example, in describing how she overcame her initial reluctance to the crime, Penny said, "I used to [feel bad] at the beginning, but then it was just like fuck it. I'm sick." Other offenders explained that these simple but powerful expressions were an indication of the mental state required to commit the crime and used them to eliminate any lingering concerns about uncertainties and risks.[7] Such expressions were especially helpful for those who entered banks or stores in hopes of cashing checks or purchasing merchandise, but even those who made fraudulent purchases behind computer screens needed them at times.

In accord with previous research on persistent offenders, the identity thieves we spoke with were remarkably confident in their abilities both to profit from their crimes and to avoid contact with law enforcement. Indeed, dwelling on the risks of crime was seen as foolish. But this does not imply that they merely accepted any risks associated with stealing identities. Our interviews revealed that they actively engaged in strategies to reduce the likelihood of detection. In fact, many articulated a sense of professionalism in their development of criminal skills.

MANAGING RISK

Research on criminal decision-making has highlighted the dynamic process of risk and reward assessment. Offenders are not passive actors who idly accept the consequences of their misdeeds. Instead, they take an active approach, engaging in strategic steps to lessen the likelihood that something bad will befall them. It is widely known that criminals (of all types) use specific strategies to avoid police detection.[8] Whether it is by minimizing the number of offenses they commit, or by changing the way they commit their crimes, offenders act strategically to reduce the formal risks of their misdeeds. Drug dealers intentionally set up in locations where they can detect approaching police cars and customers that pose risk,[9] car thieves drive stolen vehicles in ways that mimic normal drivers,[10] and johns watch prostitutes for behavioral cues to determine if they are being set up for arrest or assault.[11] Although their crimes differ greatly from those just mentioned, identity thieves also use past criminal experiences, lessons learned from trusted others, and common sense to form a loose plan when committing their crimes.

Law enforcement professionals have found that crime prevention is most effective when targeting specific types of crime. In line with this pattern of thought, we detail the strategies that identity thieves used to increase their chances of successfully acquiring victims' information and absconding with money, while also reducing their chances of being detected and arrested. While it may seem that thieves have unlimited targets and innumerable possible transactions, this is not the case. Offenders were convinced, and rightfully so, that excessive activity was a sure way to bring attention to their crimes. Thus, most were careful to limit the number of fraudulent transactions; select appropriate people, places, and times for their crimes; and lessen unnecessary exposure by blending in as much as possible. It is clear that these strategies did not make them bulletproof—as all were arrested and convicted—but they remained convinced that these strategies were effective, and their success-to-failure ratios tend to support this claim. This confidence in their strategies led to a general sense of safety when stealing identities.

Reducing the Number and Amount of Transactions

To be sure, money drives identity theft. Given that fact, we might expect identity thieves to try to maximize the amount they could get from each stolen identity and each transaction made with that identity. This was seldom the case, however. Offenders recognized that trying to maximize each fraudulent transaction was detrimental to their long-term success. They might get more money in the short term, but they couldn't sustain such reckless behavior. Thus, they limited the amount and frequency of their withdrawals to reduce their vulnerability and prolong their criminal careers. Their goal was to keep transactions small enough to remain under the radar of interested authorities, while still making substantial profits. When asked how much he would attempt to obtain with a fraudulent check, Jay answered: "Oh, it depends on the company. If you made one thousand dollars in two weeks [for the company], I wouldn't go over eight hundred. Then you could do, five or six or ten a day. But once you go over that amount, you're stuck, you can't do anything. Then it's red flagged—that name and that store are red flagged. So you gotta go to something else. So why go a little higher when you can go a little lower and do a lot more?" Jay's response suggests that situational factors were important when deciding the number of fraudulent checks that should be written and the value of each one.

As you would expect, the ideal amount for a transaction varied greatly, depending on the origin of the funds. Those who defrauded banks set higher limits than those who targeted grocery or department stores, where the goal was to write the check for an amount high enough to be worth the trouble, but low enough to avoid showing identification or waiting for special approval. Anita made her money by traveling to various grocery stores and cashing fraudulent checks. She claimed to limit each check to no more than $150, because the cashiers she targeted were not required to ask for identification for these lower amounts. In describing what made her a successful identity thief, Penny mentioned the importance of not being greedy: "It sounds bad but I wouldn't go in there and spend a thousand dollars. I'd go in there and spend a couple hundred bucks. I'd go to the grocery store and write a check for cash back and get like fifty dollars cash back. I wouldn't go in there and be like, buy five hundred dollars' worth of groceries and stupid stuff like that. I wouldn't do that."

Thieves who targeted banks allowed themselves higher maximums, but still thought that limiting the amount reduced their chances of attracting unwanted attention. Sherry and her crime partners limited their withdrawals to "usually under four hundred or five hundred dollars." Similarly, Sylvia kept her transactions to "under a thousand [dollars] just so there wouldn't be no problems." Dustin relied on his past experience to determine his target amount:

> I knew that at banks, the head teller could approve your check for up to $750 right there at the teller. They didn't have to step away from the counter. I knew this because I used to work in a bank. . . . What happened was, I wouldn't do the check for more than $740, $730, somewhere around that area. If it's a company check, they never check the signatures or anything. Personal checks they do, company checks they don't.

Jay, who cashed fraudulent payroll checks, claimed that he chose the amounts of the checks based on "how much money [a worker] makes an hour and usually two-week paychecks."

In addition to reducing the amount of each transaction, thieves thought it best not to attempt too many transactions per identity. They thought that identities could get "burned up" quickly, and using them after reaching this point was too risky. As with the amount per transaction, the number of transactions per identity considered to be safe varied greatly, depending on personal preference and the type of theft. Kendra and Sheila worked with large rings of thieves who took money from existing bank accounts. They both claimed that they would draw from each account only once or twice, and would rarely exceed this limit. Fran claimed that departing from her typical routine caused her much anxiety: "We went to four banks and we're sitting in the car and I'm paranoid because we had like seventy thousand dollars from just four banks and I'm nervous. My goal was to hit it three times. If you're using big amounts go three times [then] leave it alone. I don't care how sweet it is, how good it is, after the third time, I don't want it because I'm scared something's going to happen." Breaking from this norm led to her eventual arrest, supporting her claim that there are limits to the number of times one should enter banks with the same stolen identity.

Those who fraudulently applied for new credit cards claimed to hold them for two or three months at the most, with some exceptions. Bruce claimed that he "really didn't like to keep anything more than ninety days." Dustin reported that he would keep a card "about a month or two, depending on if I took it on the road or just stayed in the area. If I took it on the road, I'd use it for six months if I wanted to."

Selecting the Right Times, Places, and People

Identity thieves who made their profits by withdrawing money from banks or fraudulently purchasing goods from commercial establishments were aware that certain times, places, and people were safer than others. They did not go to just any bank or store, at any time, when stealing. Instead, they chose times when traffic patterns were known or predictable. Some relied on busy periods to enter stores or make withdrawals from banks. Lawrence thought the best times to commit identity theft were "pay day, Fridays and Saturdays, and around income taxes." Thieves thought that heavy customer traffic (as on pay days) would decrease workers' likelihood of checking documents too closely. As Dustin explained, "If you got sufficient funds, they're going to scan it right there because especially on pay days, they're too crowded to check every little thing." Others thought that Fridays and weekends were best because of basic banking practices. Kendra explained, "On the weekends we don't worry about it because on the weekends nothing is [recorded as] withdrawn. If we went to your account on Friday, we know it's still the same amount on Saturday, so we write checks through the whole weekend."

In addition to being selective about times, many sought specific locations to reduce their chances of being detected. Some identity thieves assumed that individual businesses varied tremendously in the amount of effort expended to detect fraud. Through experience or insider knowledge, these offenders sought out vulnerable locations. Jay thought that the security at check-cashing centers and banks was too tough. He was especially concerned with security cameras. Therefore, he preferred to target grocery stores when cashing fraudulent checks.

Others thought that banks and stores all had similar security measures. Thus, to minimize their exposure, they preferred to travel to locations far from the homes of their victims and themselves. Chelsea argued that violating this rule led to her arrest. As she explained, "if I wouldn't have worked in my area I wouldn't have gotten caught." When asked where she went to cash checks, Emma said that she "went to Portland for the bank issues and that's a three-hour drive." As Kendra explained, "Certain areas you don't go into, because we know the people that live in that area, so if you go into that area, somebody in that branch is going to know that person and that's how you get catched, you know what I mean? You never go into that area where that person live." Sherry said, "You do go to another town. You don't go to the same town. You go to another town [in the] next county."

The majority of identity thieves claimed that they were not selective in the identities they stole. For this group, it was easier to prey on any available target than to sift through potential candidates, looking for ideal victims. Those who were selective in their targets looked for "clean" names, good credit, and physical similarities between the victim and the person who assumed that identity in banks or stores. When we asked Dustin to describe a "clean" name, it triggered this exchange:

DUSTIN: Somebody like yours. I'm not saying that to be funny. I'm really not. She's looking at me like, "Oh, no!" Somebody like y'all. You've never been convicted, you probably only have one or two speeding tickets in your life. You ain't got no criminal record. Ain't nobody looking for you. You ain't wanted for child support. Stuff like that.

HEITH: Would it matter age, race, sex, anything like that?

DUSTIN: Yeah, it would. I'd give [my co-offender] an age range because they have to be somewhere around my age, preferably. I wouldn't know anything about employment history or anything like that, but as long as the NCIC [National Crime Information Center] was clean. You got a speeding ticket or two, I can deal with that, but you just have to be clean.

Another offender used similar criteria when selecting his targets: "Professionals, somebody who's stable within their job, at least ten years. That was hard to find. You had to go through a lot of identities to find that. Just someone who stayed in their part of the country and they also didn't have an extravagant credit bureau. They had maybe five credit cards, maybe one or two installment loans, they didn't have a propensity to have a lavish lifestyle. . . . Just somebody that was fairly stable." Kate preferred to target those with good credit scores instead of those with similar physical characteristics, claiming that she "didn't take anybody's credit report that wasn't over eight hundred."

In addition to targeting specific kinds of victims, a handful of thieves claimed that they preyed on certain types of bank tellers and store clerks. Much like robbers, they looked for people who would be least likely to cause them trouble.[12] Gladys detailed the characteristics she looked for in bank tellers.

HEITH: Would you try to pick specific types of tellers, like would you look for more men over women?

GLADYS: You didn't want the older ones.

HEITH: You don't want the older ones?

GLADYS: No, they've been around. No, you don't want the older ones. More like the bubbly young ones.

HEITH: What about race? Would you look for white ones over black ones?

GLADYS: It didn't matter. I kind of steered away from Orientals, Asians.

HEITH: How come?

GLADYS: Because they're too suspicious. It's true. That's how I felt about it.

HEITH: You didn't care if it was male or female?

GLADYS: No. The only ones I pretty much steered away from is Asians and the older ones.

Similarly, Fran targeted younger clerks when cashing fraudulent checks because "older people are more focused. Teenagers, talk to them long enough and they attention goes somewhere else." When asked which type of employee she preferred to approach, Emma, who was in her forties during her crimes, replied:

EMMA: Okay, you don't go to African American people because they seem to be a little more savvy on picking out who's trying to do identity theft. Young people are not quite as aware and they talk to older persons with more respect and such, so I would try to go to a clerk who looked like the work was really busy or if it was a really busy time at the store, things like that.

HEITH: Do you prefer men over women?

EMMA: Probably men, and again I would kind of be talking with them while I'm doing things. They aren't maybe paying as close attention to things.

Interestingly, these thieves did not agree on what types of employees made the best targets. Their decisions appeared to be based on personal biases and assumptions more than on sound facts. Regardless, they thought that these strategies in selecting targets aided in their success.

Blending In

Whether making transactions online or in places of commerce, identity thieves must be able to convince others that they are who they claim to be. When appearing in person, the ability to manage impressions—to communicate to observers that all is normal—is vital for their success. Many of the identity thieves we interviewed stressed the importance of looking the part when entering banks or department stores. Jay forged checks from medical companies; thus, he argued, "You gotta put your scrubs on and your pins and your stethoscope." Danny said that dressing appropriately "was part of the whole scam. When I go to check-cashing places and into the banks and everything, if it's landscaping or construction, I dress like that—like I just got paid. Got my hard hat, my utility belt, the whole nine yards. That's what I did. You know, I'm a scammer." Fran abstained from going into banks herself because she thought it too risky. She did, however, make sure that her runners dressed appropriately.

> I knew if you're going in a bank and you're going to cash a check you dressed accordingly. I always made them dress accordingly. If you're going in to cash an insurance check, [you] want to be dressed nice and casual. If you were cashing a payroll check, you got to wear a uniform. I always try to find a uniform that match whatever company we were using. With the lab tech, we went right to the uniform shop and got the little nurse scrub sets and everything.

Using a similar logic, those who targeted department stores adjusted their wardrobe as necessary. Describing how she dressed while shopping with someone else's credit card, Gladys said, "If I'm going into a jewelry store, and it's a beautiful jewelry store, I ain't going to go in there looking ghetto fabulous."

From these accounts, it is clear that identity thieves deliberately planned to resemble ordinary customers. This idea is best expressed by Joel's description of how one should look when entering banks, "you have to look the part, and act the part, and be the part." Offenders realized that to blend in does not mean to hide or appear furtive; instead, "it is to be present but of no concern."[13] Dressing the part and controlling their emotions were two important ways for achieving this goal.

Regardless of which strategies offenders used, their ultimate aim was to reduce their visibility. The less they were noticed, the greater their chances of evading detection. This belief is likely the reason many thieves considered entering banks and stores as the riskiest part of the crime. When asked if he ever went into banks himself, Lawrence, who worked with a team of other thieves, said, "No, I never do that. I don't have the nerves." Joel said, "The riskiest part? Getting the money out [of banks] because you never knew when one of those checks was going to come back bad. . . . Every time I went in I took a chance, every single time." Emma thought that "the bank is scary. It's a confined area. . . . That was very scary." Recognition of the risks of interaction explains why those who committed their crimes as part of a group often delegated the task of entering banks and stores to others.

DEVELOPING A PORTFOLIO OF SKILLS

Many contemporary criminologists portray criminals as unskilled actors who simply respond to opportunities. To these analysts, crime occurs because a willing offender sees money left on a table, a car unlocked, or a desired object unguarded. They assume that anyone with a criminal inclination (and the ability to ignore consequences) can commit the crime, with no specific skills necessary. However, ethnographic research on con men, thieves, and hustlers suggests that they do indeed have a "portfolio of skills" that is developed and improved with experience—and that this portfolio is different for those without a lengthy criminal history.[14] Persistent burglars learn to assess a home's risks and its value, experienced crack dealers and prostitutes learn to discern undercover officers, and seasoned hustlers learn to recognize and exploit new opportunities that law-abiding folk simply don't see.[15] Like these other types of offenders, identity thieves also exhibited a common portfolio of skills, a sort of "working personality."[16] These include intuitive skills, technical skills, social skills, system knowledge, and courage.

Intuitive Skills

Many of the thieves we interviewed claimed to possess a heightened intuitive ability to make sense of a situation, an awareness of their surroundings that was more developed than the average person's. Scholars have observed that criminals require the ability to "be observant and sensitive to circumstances and opportunities for illicit gain, and know when to take advantage of them and when to desist."[17] They have referred to such intuitive ability as "larceny sense," "grift sense," or "intuitive sense."[18] While discussing the occasions when she decided to postpone a crime by backing out of a bank or retail store, April revealed, "You kind of get, I don't know, almost like you dreaded walking into it." Connie described it as a "gut feeling." When asked how he improved his skills at identity theft, Bruce responded confidently:

> Sensing. Sensing what was going on within a situation, like at a bank, like I could sense what was going on with tellers. I could tell how they were looking at the screen, how long they were looking at it and I could sense whether something had been written or if I was cashing too many checks. Just a sense of how people react in situations and then also just the situations themselves. As many [situations that] presented themselves, I would find a way around them. So I guess just honing the thinking on your feet.

Danny's response underscores this reliance on intuition: "You just kind of knew [when] something was not right. . . . I just knew. I mean it's just you would get a knack for it. Once you been in this game awhile, you know when something isn't right."

Several offenders believed that they would not have been caught if they had paid closer attention to their premonitions. For instance, Kendra described the moments before she was arrested: "I knew the detectives were watching. I knew that and I had the feeling and I told [my codefendant] but he was trying to kick heroin that day. And this stupid fool was shooting [heroin] and I'm all surrounded by [people] smoking meth and smoking weed. . . . And I told him, I said we got to leave. I have this freaking feeling something's going to go wrong." Similarly, Sheila claimed to sense a bad omen, which she regretfully ignored, on the day she was arrested: "When I walked in [the bank] and actually stumbled as I walked through the door, and lost my shoe, and [laughs] I knew something was wrong. And that happened to be the day that I got busted."

Most thieves were unable to clearly articulate what they meant by intuition. When pressed, they appeared to describe an ability to assess risk and recognize opportunity based on experience. They felt that their prior thefts (and attempted thefts) had given them the ability to "read" situations and act accordingly. Absent any warning signs, offenders claimed to feel safe, which then allowed them to remain confident. But this does not mean that identity thieves in general truly have a better intuitive sense of danger than those who abstain from crime. Much of what the thieves described as intuitive skill was little more than common sense. Moreover, even those who are adept in social situations may falter when faced with the anxiety of a stressful situation. It was in such situations that practice and experience, coupled with a naturally calm demeanor, helped alleviate anxiety and allowed many of these seasoned thieves to present themselves as legitimate customers. Doubtless, those who continuously play high-stakes games are better able to keep their bearings and monitor their surroundings than those who are criminal novices.

Technical Skills

Regardless of the development of their "larceny sense" or how adept they were in social interactions, identity thieves acknowledged that, to be successful, they had to possess a minimal level of technical skills or have the necessary contacts with those who did. These included the abilities to produce fraudulent documents, identification cards, and checks—none of which are easy tasks. Continually evolving measures to combat fraud have made it increasingly difficult to commit document forgery. Gone are the days when fraudsters like Frank Abagnale could simply laminate stock paper to create suitable identification, or forgers could produce counterfeit checks with readily available materials.[19] Modern checks and identification cards require offenders to replicate watermarks, magnetic strips, and multiple ink colors.

While many identity thieves obtained their forged documents from other sources, a sizable number learned these tricks themselves, through experimentation and practice. Kendra described how she learned to create realistic documents: "We studied IDs. Then I went to the stamp shop, the paint shop, and got the logos right. I know the [bank name] was one of the hardest banks for us to get money out, but when I found out about the logos, when I passed it through the black light, it became real easy. . . . I went to the stamp shop and bought a stamp and sat there for hours and hours with the colors and I made like seven different IDs before it come through under the black light."

Lawrence described how he produced fraudulent checks: "I use a different type of paper. The paper always came straight from the bank. A lot of people, they would get paper out of like Target or Office Max or places like that. That kind of paper right there, it's not always efficient. Nine times out of ten, the bank may stop it. They want to check the company payroll." Besides the right paper stock, thieves needed additional equipment to replicate checks and identification documents.

Those who produced fraudulent documents took pride in their skills and the effort they expended to master their techniques. When asked if he made fake checks, Dustin replied: "It wasn't just a fake. You don't call it a fake check. You call it a perfect duplication. No, seriously though, with technology today, the way computers and printers are, I can look at your University of Alabama paycheck and make one just like it because companies now sell the software where you can actually print the checks. When you do it with the intent to do something, you research it. You know the little numbers down on the bottom, those have to be used with magnetic ink now because they scan and everything. Things you just know." A similar sense of pride emerges in the following conversation with Joel:

JOEL: I mean it took me time to perfect my Social Security cards. I didn't know that there was a watermark on them, or watermarks on them, different colors. I don't know if you've ever really looked at them, but if you look at your Social Security card you're gonna see these little red, yellow, and blue dots all over

them. You know, it comes up on the scanner, so I didn't know
that until I really started looking, so there were times where . . .

HEITH: So, did you get turned away a lot?

JOEL: No.

HEITH: Never?

JOEL: Twice. And I've gotten my identities in Tennessee, Louisi-
ana, Missouri, Iowa, North Dakota, South Dakota, Colorado,
New Mexico, trying to give you the states, Wyoming, Kansas,
Oklahoma, Minnesota, and a bunch of others. . . . In Missouri
I had five and New Mexico I had four.

Without a doubt, identity thieves need specific abilities and
skills to replicate cards and documents. But with improvements in
technology, artistic ability is no longer required. With persistence,
and the proper equipment, almost anyone can master the art of
counterfeiting, at least to the degree needed to fool most people.

Social Skills

Most frauds and cons require that offenders be adept at presenting themselves as honest and trustworthy. To allay suspicion
and put would-be victims at ease, thieves often must be sensitive
to others' concerns and respond to emerging interpersonal problems. In other words, fraudsters must possess good social skills.
The ability to manipulate a social situation, through both verbal
and non-verbal communication, was perhaps the most important
skill that identity thieves claimed to possess. As Dustin explained,
"I can manipulate a situation. That's what I'm saying. It was about
finesse."

At the most basic level, to pass as their intended victims, identity thieves must be able to impersonate legitimate customers in
stores and banks. To ward off unwanted suspicion or resistance,
they had to be able to represent a larcenous situation as an ordinary one and remove any doubts about its illegitimacy. As part of
this process, thieves used deference and respect, were chatty and
friendly, acted naive and puzzled, or exhibited confidence and as-

sertiveness, depending on the situation. In describing what it was like to interact with bank and store employees, Bruce, an experienced thief, said, "You definitely have to be adaptable. It's not even being pleasant with people. It's just having authority. You have to have authority of whatever situation you are in. And if you have that authority, people will not go any farther than to peripherally question you. That's about it." Emma explained, "I would just act as if I were that person and I would go in and I'd be talking to the person processing the application and, say if it were at Home Depot, I would be saying, 'Oh, we're doing some remodeling of our home' or something like that and I'd engage the people." It was not better-than-average social skills that allowed these thieves to be successful. It was the fact that they could maintain these skills in highly stressful, anxiety-inducing situations—this is the ability that most law-abiding citizens do not possess.

Offenders claimed that their skills in manipulating others were especially important in non-routine situations. When describing how she conducted herself in a bank when questioned by employees, Tameka said, "If it was a tricky question you should be able to talk to the bank manager because there were times when I asked to speak to the manager if I was withdrawing a large sum of money. In essence you had to become these people [the victims]." Fran argued that you had to have "a real manipulative spirit when you're doing this. You have to be conniving and manipulative to convince people to do what you want [them] to do."

In addition to verbally controlling a situation, offenders acknowledged that they also had to display the symbols of legitimacy. As discussed earlier, this included dressing in the manner of people who "belonged." As Gladys noted, "I mean I can go into a place knowing how to look the part. You go up to a place and you look in there and get the feeling about how a person would look. I'd take off a ring or something, put on a ring, take off some of your make-up, or go put on a hat or a scarf, put some glasses on." Through her ability to assess the situation and adapt accordingly, Gladys and others like her could better manipulate the situation to their benefit than could people with limited experience with crime.

Appropriate dress went hand in hand with the ability to present one's self as legitimate, to "talk your way to the person so they don't feel suspicious." In this respect, persistent identity thieves resemble portrayals of con men who "cultivated the social side more than any other criminal group. They are able to fit in unobtrusively on any social level."[20]

System Knowledge

The identity thieves in our sample also described the need to have a basic knowledge of how stores, banks, and credit agencies operated. For most offenders, their ordinary banking experiences—opening legitimate accounts, applying for credit—were enough. As Sherry explained, "You have to have an idea of how banks work. At some point in your life, live a normal life and understand how credit is extended and things like that." But more sophisticated types of crimes required more specialized knowledge. According to Carlos:

> Well you definitely have to know how loans work. You have to know how title companies, funding companies, banks in general work. Then on top of that you have to be pretty adept with computers, [know] how to pull a program apart. And I don't mean in code, but how to really operate a program. . . . You got to know how all of that works. So, yeah, there's some skills you definitely have to have and you really got to know the rules. I think that's a lot of what people don't really get is that it's easier, everything is easier than you think, if you know the rules.

Some learned this insider information from legitimate employment at the types of places they defrauded. Kate claimed that "if I didn't have my background information in insurance, I would have never ever, ever have thought of doing this." Earlier, we mentioned Dustin's acknowledgment that his prior employment at a bank taught him the maximum amount of money a check could be cashed for without managerial approval.

At a more local level, thieves had to learn which neighborhood businesses were most easily defrauded and which should be left alone. This included knowing which stores had more liberal check-cashing policies, such as accepting checks without identification. As Penny explained, "You can go to [department store name] and write a check with no ID because they don't require you to show an ID under a certain amount. If the check goes through, they won't [ask for an ID], unless the machine tells them to." According to our interviewees, certain stores were known for taking checks with minimal hassle and others for granting credit with few background checks. Knowing how individual banks, stores, and credit agencies operated allowed offenders to minimize risks and maximize gains. Penny claimed that she liked targeting specific department and grocery stores because "they are the easiest ones and you can get cash back." This type of local knowledge could be learned through routine business transactions, or from other identity thieves willing to share information.

Courage

Those who commit crime are often beset by fear and paranoia; these intense negative emotions are enough to prevent most of us from engaging in crime of any kind. The offenders we interviewed claimed that it was necessary to have certain psychological predispositions when engaging in identity theft. One of the most important was "heart" or courage. This was especially true for those who entered banks or stores and interacted directly with people, which most thieves contended was the riskiest part of the crime. Tameka best explained this idea: "H-E-A-R-T [she spells it out]. You had to have a lot of guts to go in and ask for it. [laughs] 'Cause I went in with security guards—there can be a guard standin' there—and I spoke to them too. 'Good mornin' sir, how are you?'"

Dustin described it this way:

> I've had bank robbers tell me, people convicted of bank robbery, and I never will understand this, say that I had more heart to walk into a bank with a ten-thousand-dollar check than it took them to walk in there with a gun and get twenty-five hundred to three thousand. I never understood that. They said it takes more heart to

do what I do than to do what they do because theirs is just spur of the moment. That gun is all of the authority that you need. You see a gun pointed at your face and you going to give them everything. But me, I'm walking in there unarmed and coming out with three times more money than they are.

Of course, some may question this claim that identity theft requires more courage than crimes that require direct confrontation and threats of violence. For example, the possibility that a victim will fight back is always present during robberies, but rarely during identity theft. In fact, none of those we interviewed mentioned being physically attacked in the process of their crimes. Regardless of Dustin's anecdote, however, it is clear that entering a business with the intent to defraud requires a certain psychological disposition.

We do not wish to portray identity thieves as having special gifts or an innate ability to commit fraud. Instead, we find that identity thieves have developed a general portfolio of skills that are useful for locating personal information, converting it into cash or goods, and avoiding law enforcement. For seasoned offenders, the development of these skills can instill the courage and confidence needed to overcome risks and continue to commit their crimes.

PERSONAL SKILL ASSESSMENTS AND EXPLANATIONS OF ARREST

Those who said they had the necessary skills to successfully steal identities were quite confident in their abilities; perhaps overly so. It was not uncommon for them to boast about their unique abilities, the ones that separated them from "run of the mill" identity thieves. Bruce claimed that he was "very good," adding, "I was never captured by any place. There were no institutions to capture me or could [have] or have been able to." Lawrence reported, "I thought I was real good. . . . I thought I was a beast. I thought I was an animal." Jay argued that not everyone is good at crime or identity theft, but he was. In his words, "you get good at it real quick or you don't ever get good at it. Most of them weren't. I got good at it real quick." According to Danny, his crimes were a "calculated risk" and he "never worried about getting caught . . . because that's how quick and good I was." Such bold confidence was remarkably common among the thieves in our sample.

One will likely question why these offenders held their skills in such high esteem, in light of the fact that they all had been caught and incarcerated for their offenses. The answer is simple—they located the blame for their arrests elsewhere. Their excuses and explanations included the departure from a tried-and-true method, dumb luck on the part of the police, and the failings of others.

Several thieves claimed that their capture occurred because they simply got sloppy, deviating from plans that had worked in the past. When asked why she thought she got caught, Tameka replied, "We didn't use the pattern this time." Likewise, Bruce insisted that he was caught only because he went off script, violating his own policy of not stealing the identities of friends. As he explained, "I think at the time I had quite a few homes and quite a few cars and the bills were coming due on everything and I had slacked off for about two months about not getting any money. So I was in pinch to get the money to pay for the lifestyle I had. I had friends in all of these areas and there was upkeep on stuff. I didn't want it to all go down, so I took the risk of doing this. And it was not the right thing to do."

Other offenders claimed that it was not a lack of skill or planning that led to their arrest, but merely chance. As Dale revealed, "It's always bad luck that gets you caught. You don't get caught in the store; you don't get caught in the bank. . . . I've never been apprehended in the bank or department store." Dustin claimed his arrest stemmed from a simple traffic stop.

DUSTIN: I didn't know that [a town in] Georgia had a misdemeanor warrant on me for writing a bad check, so I got stopped in Jacksonville—it's right across the line. [Police] said, "They got a hold on you, man, for a bad check. We got to take you back there." So I'm sitting up there in the county jail on a misdemeanor hearing and here comes the postal inspectors.
HEITH: What'd the cop pull you over for?

DUSTIN: Just for a regular traffic violation. But there was other
things going on in Jacksonville that they figured that since I
was out it might be me. There was a whole lot of counterfeiting done and the Secret Service knew that my trade was really
counterfeiting and they figuring since [I was] out, I've got to be
doing this.

When asked how she got caught, Penny gave a similar answer:
"Random. Just pulled us over because the girl didn't have tags on
her car." According to her, the warrant for her arrest was issued because of her association with another person (who had committed
a robbery). In another story of so-called bad luck, police officers
initially came to Alisha's home to arrest her and her roommates for
methamphetamine production. While searching the house, they
also found evidence of identity theft.

Twelve participants in our sample explained that their careers
in identity theft would have continued unabated—were it not for
others in their group, people who lacked the proper skills or who
turned on them after being caught. Lawrence claimed that it was
the introduction of partners to his schemes that led to his downfall. "Actually, when I was doing things by myself I was pretty good.
When I started bringing other people into it, people that's close to
me, and getting them to finding people to do things, that's when I
messed up." Kate reported that "the FBI agent said that if it wasn't
for [an informant] that they never ever would have caught me. And
they know that I've done more but they never, they never could
prove it and I wasn't going to tell them anything. [laughs] So basically, that's where it all came about." Jeannette blamed her arrest
on her ex-husband. When asked why he informed on her, she said,
"Spite. Because he wasn't winning what he wanted out of the divorce. He wanted out of the marriage with me getting nothing and
that wasn't going to happen and I was going to get fifty percent
because we were married for thirty-one years." When asked how
she got caught, Fran said, "My codefendant that cooperated with
them, she got caught on passing a check. If I'm not mistaken, it was
. . . for a thousand dollars, for a computer. And she got caught on

that case and just scared her or what, but she just started telling them everything she was involved in and that caused them to start an investigation on us."

It should be noted that several offenders offered multiple explanations of their arrests and convictions. For example, Kendra's response incorporated all of the previous excuses into a single account. She claimed that her partners "got very careless towards the end. . . . Everybody was getting high and getting careless and getting greedy." When asked to explain how they got careless, she said, "Well, some of the codefendants were going into the banks by themselves because they needed the money. They would do it by themselves without me knowing." Thus, as Kendra saw it, greedy partners began changing their ordinarily reliable plans. They were arrested due to foolish mistakes, then became informants to cut deals with the police. In her mind, her only mistake was not controlling her partners better.

THEORETICAL AND POLICY IMPLICATIONS

The past few decades have witnessed a dramatic decrease in crime rates throughout the United States. Scholars have offered numerous explanations for the drop in crime, including the stabilization of drug markets, increased incarceration rates, an aging population, and innovative strategies implemented by police.[1] More recently, some have suggested that a decline in the use of cash may be partly responsible for the decrease in property crimes.[2] With fewer people carrying cash, and stricter limits on the amounts of cash that stores keep on premises, there are simply fewer opportunities for would-be robbers and burglars to find scores worth their time. Interestingly, this nationwide drop in property crimes corresponded with an increase in white-collar crimes, such as fraud and identity theft.[3] It is estimated that more than 11 million adult consumers were victims of identity theft in 2009, an increase from nearly 10 million in 2008.[4] Moreover, data from the 2009 Consumer Sentinel Network report indicate that identity theft was the top complaint category for the 2008 calendar year—comprising 26 percent of complaints overall—and it has been ranked number one for several previous years.[5]

Such high rates of victimization likely have contributed to the public's concern for the security and privacy of their personal information. The findings from a survey of U.S. residents suggests that nearly two-thirds of respondents reported that they are either "extremely" or "very" concerned about identity theft and credit and debit card fraud.[6] Additionally, survey research indicates that from 40 to 66 percent of citizens would be willing to pay extra taxes (about eighty-seven dollars annually) if the money were used to help guard against identity theft.[7]

As a result of these concerns, citizens have changed the way they manage financial accounts and protect their personal information.[8] Many have begun purchasing—for sizable fees—various products and programs designed to protect them from victimization, including credit monitoring, fraud alerts, and information monitoring. Industry reports have shown that more consumers use credit monitoring services than any other identity theft protection product, with three out of ten consumers enrolled as of year-end 2008.[9] In fact, credit monitoring services alone are approaching $1 billion in sales each year, as millions of people have signed up.[10] Another indication of consumers' fear of identity theft—and their increasing vigilance in protecting their information—is the sudden popularity of paper shredders. Sales of personal shredders have shown double-digit percentage increases over the past few years, and shredders are the fastest-growing segment of the total office products market.[11]

Although reports from public and private agencies that collect data on identity theft indicate that it is growing both more common and more costly, researchers have devoted little attention to studying those who engage in this crime. Much has been written on victim characteristics, prevention techniques, and emerging legislation. Until now, however, there has not been a systematic examination of offenders. This book's goal was to begin filling this gap in our knowledge. By assessing the perspectives of offenders, we hoped to produce a more comprehensive picture of identity theft; a picture that would offer suggestions for how this crime might be better controlled.

Our interpretation of the accounts provided by identity thieves was guided by contemporary rational choice theory. Although our aim was not to test the predictive ability or explanatory power of rational choice theory, we drew upon insights from this theory to shape the structure of our interviews, make sense of what the offenders said, and organize our findings. As a result, we imply in much of our writing that identity thieves were rational, at least to some degree, in their decisions to become involved in identity theft, in their assessments of risk and their attempts to manage that risk, and in how they chose to enact their crimes. Other theories could have been used to guide the interpretation of these same interviews. In fact, we borrowed from a variety of other theories to supplement our analysis, including differential association and the sociology of accounts. Nevertheless, after thinking about the interviews throughout the research process, we concluded that applying the elements of rational choice theory was the most effective approach for making sense of the data.

Before discussing the theoretical relevance of our findings, we think it important to acknowledge that we do not suggest that identity thieves are always cautious, rational actors who carefully weigh the costs and benefits of criminal conduct and compare it to other lines of action. We recognize that much of their behavior—before, during, and after the crime—was haphazard and improvisational, spawned by a sense of desperation. However, this caveat should not be taken to mean that no thought and planning were involved in their decisions. Many criminal decisions that seem haphazard or thoughtless to an outsider may in fact be the result of experience and expertise.[12] Identity thieves' perceptions and beliefs about the characteristics of desirable victims, or effective risk-reduction strategies, were likely to have been developed through experience or under the tutelage of other offenders. Offenders did not set out to maximize their returns on each stolen identity. Instead, they relied on convenience, experience, and casual familiarity with their crimes to minimize risk and increase rewards. When situations and targets closely matched their perceived ideals, they seized the opportunity to offend.

CRIMINAL PERSISTENCE

The past few decades have seen a dramatic increase in the number of studies devoted to understanding the development and maintenance of "criminal careers."[13] The concept of criminal careers is a theoretical tool for analyzing the various stages of a person's history with crime. Such careers consist of three stages: initiation, persistence, and desistance.[14] In other words, offenders must first decide when they are ready to commit a crime, whether they should continue committing crime and, eventually, whether they should stop committing crime altogether. This research has revealed the various background factors and situational inducements that attract people to crime, encourage them to persist, and eventually turn their heads away from crime.[15] For example, we know that military service, steady employment, and marriage all contribute to an offender's decision to give up on crime.[16] As important as it is to understand the factors that lead one to desist, it is equally essential to understand those that contribute to persistence.[17]

Much of our analysis has focused on the factors that led identity thieves to consider their crimes financially rewarding and relatively risk-free, which ultimately encouraged them to continue offending. This mental calculation of costs and benefits is a subjective process, in which the relevant variables are constantly reassessed. With experience (and the subsequent cognitive re-interpretations), risks that seemed insurmountable on one day can be overlooked on the next. Correspondingly, rewards that once were thought negligible can eventually, under new circumstances, turn offenders' heads. Improved skills and professionalism, changing risk assessments, eroding financial resources, and reliance on linguistic devices such as justifications and excuses act in concert to foster images of identity theft as being a more rational choice than it once was (or actually is).

By developing a sense of professionalism and refining their skills with acquiring information, converting it to cash or goods, and avoiding arrest, identity thieves increased their chances of being successful at crime. (Or at least many believed this to be the case.) The self-perceived mastery of their craft may be why so few feared detection or the legal consequences if captured. Those who have committed offenses with impunity have overly optimistic views of their crimes,[18] which was the case for many of those we interviewed. Offenders came to believe that they could continue offending by relying on their skills in evading capture, thereby nullifying the deterrent effects of criminal sanctions. Each successful theft reinforced not only their belief that identity theft was easy, but also their confidence in avoiding arrest, by what many perceived as inferior law enforcement. Despite being arrested and convicted for their crimes, the majority of them still maintained that they were skilled thieves. Their arrests were attributed to bad luck, sloppiness, or snitching rather than their own failings.

Improved professionalism and skills also made the commission of crime more palatable to offenders by reducing the fear and anxiety that often accompany felonious activities. Interviews with street-level property offenders suggest that fear and anxiety are the overriding emotions during the commission of a crime.[19] To persist in their crimes, offenders must learn to manage these intense emotions, while maintaining some minimal level of composure. This can be a daunting task. For many people, the anxiety, fear, and paranoia that accompany crime are enough to deter them from this risky behavior. While some offenders have the ability to push these fears out of their minds when committing a crime,[20] walking into a bank with a fraudulent check and forged identification can cause even the most seasoned offender to become riddled with fear and panic. By relying on their elevated perceptions of their own skills, and thinking of identity theft as a low-risk activity, identity thieves gained the peace of mind that comes from having control over a situation. In addition, some interpreted the emotions generated by their crimes as positive experiences. What those with less criminal experience or inclination might interpret as fear and anxiety, they characterized as a rush of excitement. Such strategies made any remaining negative emotions easier to overcome and facilitated criminal persistence.

Their eroding access to legitimately secured funds, diminishing contact with or support from conventional friends and family, and efforts to maintain a lifestyle that might include drug use or addiction, led many offenders to perceive identity theft as a viable way to forestall or reverse uncomfortable situations. The fact that the cash-intensive lifestyle of most street-level identity thieves could not be sustained by legitimate employment may have undermined both the inclination and ability to hold a job, except in those cases where that employment afforded them the opportunities to carry out their crimes. Even if many offenders were willing to work at the kinds of employment available to them, and evidence suggests that they were not, the physical and temporal demands of work conflicted with their lifestyles. For example, few people can spend the night drinking in clubs, then arise routinely the next morning for work. And from a purely practical perspective, the best times of day for cashing fraudulent checks or appropriating victims' money are the times when most workers are on the job; days spent searching for suitable banks or information on potential victims cannot be spent at the office. Consequently, many of those who pursued identity theft left their legitimate employment. The absence of lawful income thus reinforced the need to find other sources of money. In these contexts, the decision to persist in identity theft could seem reasonable, if not rational.

Finally, the use of linguistic devices allowed offenders to free themselves from the guilt or negative self-image that they otherwise might have associated with their crimes. Although neutralization theory was originally used to explain initiation into delinquent behavior, some argue that neutralization theory is best understood as an explanation of criminal persistence or desistance.[21] Neutralizations might start as after-the-fact rationalizations, but later become the rationale or moral-release mechanisms that facilitate future offending.[22] Travis Hirschi describes the acceptance of neutralizations as part of a "hardening process" that advances criminal careers.[23] Ronald Akers reaches a similar conclusion in his discussion of the "definitions" favorable to crime: "Initial acts may and do occur in the absence of definitions favorable to them; rather the definitions get applied retroactively to excuse or redefine the initial deviant acts. To the extent that they successfully mitigate others' or self-punishment, they become discriminative for repetition of the deviant acts and, hence, precede the future commission of the acts."[24] Thus, by holding onto these justifications or excuses—and bringing them to the foreground when needed—thieves can continue a line of behavior without the corresponding guilt or loss of status. Whether such neutralizations affect their initial participation in identity theft is unclear, but a reliance on these techniques does appear to have helped them continue with their crimes.

Restrictive Deterrence

Our findings also have implications for another theory that falls under the umbrella of rational choice: restrictive deterrence. Criminologists often portray street offenders as unskilled actors who take advantage of found opportunities with little planning or forethought. This image of disorganized offenders is rooted partly in ethnographic research, which has documented that offenders seldom calculate long-term or formal risks when deciding to commit crime.[25] Indeed, the accounts of offenders, including those with whom we spoke, show that formal risks are easily dismissed. Offenders appear to focus on satisfying immediate needs or desires, rather than worrying about potential criminal penalties. This "here and now" outlook constrains offenders' subjective assessments of the risks and rewards of crime, often making criminal behavior appear more rewarding than it actually is.[26]

We should not take these findings to suggest that all crime, including identity theft, lacks a rational element. Ethnographic research also reveals that offenders are influenced by the situational risks of crime after a decision to offend has been reached. Dustin's words reflect this orientation: "From a criminal standpoint, you never think about getting caught because you know that the end is going to come soon. The thing is you try to minimize your exposure to the crime." The focus of much offending then, is not on whether committing crime is risky, but on how to reduce immediate risks when committing specific criminal acts. Such admissions imply reasoning offenders who think strategically, evaluate opportunities, and design their crimes to reduce risks and increase success, rather than passive actors who are simply at the mercy of threats from formal and informal sources. This idea is consistent with recent work on restrictive deterrence, which examines how offenders perceive and manage the situational risks of crime commission.[27]

Restrictive deterrence focuses on "strategies or tactics employed by individuals to evade detection, identification, or apprehension" as well as probabilistic notions of how selective and active one should be to commit crime successfully.[28] Because most strategies and tactics often include rules of thumb about certain criminal situations that should be avoided, the result of applying such strategies is a reduction in the frequency of offenses.[29] As restrictive deterrence implies, offenders do not commit all or even most of the crimes that they consider. Instead, they look for particular places and victims that are deemed suitable. When the characteristics of a situation are unsuitable, offenders find it difficult to act. Conversely, offenders may find it difficult to reject criminal opportunities that meet or approximate their conception of a situation containing acceptable risks and rewards. In a given context, the same mental process that restricts action can inspire it.

The accounts provided by identity thieves lend support to this notion of restrictive deterrence. The potential for detection and arrest was nearly always present for these offenders. They knew that avoiding arrest involved more than leaving a bank or store with money in hand. The nature of their crimes lends itself to prolonged investigations by law enforcement. They could be arrested at any time. In fact, several mentioned that they were arrested many months after committing their crimes. Some even claimed that they had already abandoned identity theft by the time they were picked up by police. This awareness of the potential delay in arrest made identity thieves cognizant of the need to take steps to minimize their visibility, both when committing their crimes and when out in public in general.

As we discussed in chapter 4, identity thieves did not seek to maximize their potential gains by getting the most money possible from each stolen identity. Instead, they exercised restraint, limiting both the number of transactions made with each identity and the amount withdrawn during each transaction. Fearing that overusing an account or attempting to withdraw too much cash would bring unwanted attention to their activities, they often left money on the table, so to speak. They also did not exploit every promising identity that they stole. Many took care to locate particularly suitable identities, even though this meant more effort, smaller profits, and delays in reaping any reward. Finally, thieves were aware that too much fraudulent activity in their own hometowns and those of their victims could be damaging to their long-term success. Many made trips to other towns or states to avoid detection.

By offenders' own accounts, these risk-reducing strategies decreased the total number of frauds committed. In fact, some identity thieves were careful to take time off between successful frauds in an attempt to reduce their overall exposure. Although these results support restrictive deterrence, ironically, such behaviors also may be instrumental in the persistence of their criminal careers, as engaging in these strategies may not only have helped them avoid arrest, but also reinforced the notion that continuing to offend is a reasonable decision. Thus, although identity thieves' avoidance strategies may reduce the number of offenses in the short term, they may, in the long run, allow more fraudulent activity to occur.

Again, we do not wish to oversell the degree of rationality and professionalism exhibited by identity thieves or the effectiveness of their arrest avoidance strategies. After all, every participant in our interviews had been incarcerated for identity theft. Nevertheless, those who used these strategies believed them to be effective. When evidence to the contrary was mentioned, they deflected blame for their incarcerations elsewhere (departing from established plans, snitches, dumb luck, or persistent law enforcement) or claimed not to have used the proper strategies in the particular case that led to their arrest. The absolute effectiveness of their strategies, however, may not be important. The fact that the use of these techniques reduces offenders' overall numbers of identity thefts still supports the tenets of restrictive deterrence.

WHAT CAN WE DO TO STOP THEM?

All crime-control programs are based on assumptions about the nature of the target crime and the characteristics of individuals who commit it. In a perfect world, such programs would be developed and implemented after systematic data collection and analysis, rather than political agendas, hunches, or tradition. Although appropriate data with which to craft such policies can come from a variety of sources, we think the best information comes directly from the offenders. By understanding how offenders interpret their actions, recognize opportunities, and carry out their crimes, those charged with creating crime-prevention programs will have a richer knowledge base from which to develop effective policies.[30] Our descriptions of identity thieves' motivations, perceptions of risks, and social organization offer insights for law enforcement, businesses, and individuals seeking to thwart this behavior. Our suggestions for prevention incorporate several well-known, situational crime-prevention techniques, including increasing the effort the offender must use to acquire and convert information, increasing the risks of getting caught, and removing excuses that offenders may use to justify their crime.

Situational Crime Prevention

In contrast to the broad-brush methods typical of many crime-prevention programs, the past few decades have seen increasing acceptance of the need for better-focused efforts. Referred to broadly as "situational crime prevention," this approach uses tactics and strategies tailored specifically to the type of crime in question. It emphasizes measures that involve the management, design, or manipulation of the immediate environment in as systematic and permanent a way as possible to reduce the opportunities for crime and increase its risks as perceived by a wide range of offenders.[31] Grounded in rational choice theory, the logic of situational crime prevention suggests that the level of criminal activity can be reduced by manipulating features of given social situations so as to limit the potential opportunities for crime. The techniques of situational crime prevention are designed to increase the effort and risk required to secure criminal gains, reduce the potential rewards and provocations of illegal behavior, and remove ready-made excuses for committing crime.[32] To be most effective, such efforts should be focused on specific types of crime.[33]

INCREASING EFFORT AND RISK / Based on the accounts of those we interviewed, obtaining personally identifying information and entering businesses to obtain cash or goods are perceived to be the riskiest parts of identity theft. Much has already been done to make it more difficult for thieves to secure information. Media campaigns warning citizens to guard their personal information have been widespread, typically focusing on telling people to monitor their credit reports and shred documents. Perhaps one of the most comprehensive of these campaigns has been the report, *Taking Charge: Fighting Back Against Identity Theft*, made freely available by the Federal Trade Commission. Most of the suggestions contained in this report would have greatly increased the effort required by offenders in our sample to acquire victims' information, as well as reduced their chances of success. The report's suggestions include shredding all documents containing personally identifying information before disposal in trash cans, putting outgoing mail containing checks or other documents with personal information in official U.S. mailboxes rather than home mailboxes, being careful about giving information to people over the phone or Internet, and securing purses and wallets when at work or out shopping. Such campaigns are likely to be effective at increasing the effort and risk associated with identity theft.

Awareness campaigns also should warn victims of other crimes—including robbery, pickpocketing, purse snatching, and burglary—that they are at risk of identity theft as well. In addition to stealing televisions, cash, and guns, for example, a burglar also might have taken the homeowner's personally identifying information, which could then be sold to the leader of a SLIT ring. Thus, victims should be informed that, in addition to notifying their insurance company of the loss of material items, they should consider placing fraud alerts on their financial accounts and monitor their credit for any suspicious activity. The results of our interviews suggest that such measures would reduce identity theft, at least for the opportunistic offender.

In addition to encouraging individuals to protect their personal information, our interviews suggest that businesses play an important role in preventing offenders from acquiring information. A sizable amount of identity theft is the result of unsafe business practices. Many offenders stole information from the mailboxes or dumpsters of small businesses. This fact has led some to suggest that businesses which store or collect personal identifiers should maintain tighter control over their facilities (for example, use lockable mailboxes, shred all documents, and track keystrokes of computer users).[34] Additionally, businesses should make greater use of "place managers," persons who monitor key access points such as mailboxes, computer files, and trash cans. To accomplish this goal, companies could provide rewards for supervisors of employee or customer records.[35]

Programs designed to educate potential victims and improve the ways that businesses control access to information will prove ineffective, however, when that information is compromised by individuals who have legitimate access to it. Many of the offenders in our sample were able to purchase victims' personally identifying information from employees of various businesses and government agencies. We recommend that all such organizations take steps to reduce the likelihood of such breaches in information security. Strategies may include careful background checks for employees, alerting employees about the real consequences of identity theft for victims, and maintaining a positive work environment.[36] Further, limiting both the collection of personal information and the number of employees who have access to this information will help reduce opportunities for these types of thefts.[37]

While the crime-reduction strategies we have mentioned so far focus on preventing the acquisition of information, this is not the only method—or perhaps even the most effective one—for reducing the number of identity thefts. An overwhelming proportion of the thieves we spoke with said that entering banks and stores was the riskiest part of the crime. Thus, prevention efforts focused on this stage in the criminal event might be extremely effective. Banks, for example, could make simple changes in procedures that would increase both the effort and the risk of identity theft. For instance, they could require passwords to withdraw money from accounts or cash checks, even when customers engage in these transactions in person. Several offenders suggested that, had this procedure been in place, they could not have completed their fraudulent withdrawals. Clearly, this strategy would not deter those thieves who have inside partners or access to a bank's computer system. But because the majority of offenders in our sample obtained personal and banking information from strangers, it would have been very difficult (if not impossible) for them to guess their victims' passwords.

As several of our respondents mentioned, large department stores that give easy and instant credit are especially susceptible to fraud. Because identity thieves actively exploit these opportunities, stores that offer instant credit should increase security to protect their consumers. Simple changes in policy—such as confirming a credit applicant's identity, requiring a waiting period, and diligently checking identification for all credit purchases—would greatly increase the efforts and risks of these crimes. As the thieves themselves reported, store personnel often neglected to verify identification when applying for and using store credit cards.

Stores also should require identification when customers cash checks. While many identity thieves can produce fake identification, not all have that capability. This strategy will have limited effectiveness, however, unless all stores consistently check identification. Through experience and inside knowledge, identity thieves learn which stores routinely check identification and what dollar amounts require proof of identification or manager approval. If some stores do not follow these recommendations, then target displacement is likely to occur.[38] As other scholars have noted, one problem with many antitheft programs is that, "Within easy reach of every house with a burglar alarm, or car with an antitheft device, are many others without such protection."[39] Similarly, without a consistent requirement for proof of identification, too many suitable targets will remain in easy reach of offenders, undercutting the deterrent effect.

Although most of the identity thieves in our sample were adept at obtaining false documents—either by creating them themselves or hiring others to do so—authorities should continue to improve the security of such documents, making them both more resistant to tampering and more difficult to duplicate. Current programs, promoted by the government's efforts to combat domestic and international terrorism, are likely to disrupt offenders' abilities to duplicate driver's licenses, passports, and state identification cards. Many identity thieves also were skilled in the art of duplicating personal and business checks. They described how easy it was to purchase the machines, paper, software, and ink required to make checks. Controlling and tracking the sale of such items would increase the effort required of offenders to successfully convert victims' information into profit. In addition, businesses and government agencies should continue to improve the training of bank tellers, store clerks, and other employees whose work responsibilities include the verification of identification documents.

Increasing the effort and risk associated with stealing identifying information and converting it into cash or goods requires diligence on the part of individuals as well as businesses. While individuals certainly have incentives to guard their information, this is not necessarily true for businesses. Although a widely publicized data breach can become a public-relations nightmare, businesses can simply pass on the other costs of identity theft to consumers in the form of higher fees. Moreover, a company can write off losses due to identity theft as a business expense when calculating corporate income taxes. Some have suggested that, if identity theft more directly impacted the bottom line, businesses would be more likely to take precautions against it.[40] Thus, in addition to encouraging individuals to protect their information, regulatory officials should take more steps to hold financial institutions accountable. This should include mandatory reporting of identity theft and those frauds associated with using stolen information, as well as changes to corporate tax laws. By implementing mandatory reporting, we could obtain more reliable data on the number and nature of identity theft incidents that occur each year. One possible use of this data might be consumer reports on businesses that employ best practices and maintain low rates of theft (or, conversely, those that are less careful with customers' information). In a free-market economy, sanctions that target the bottom line—either through tax policy or consumer education—may encourage institutions to take more precautions against identity theft.[41]

STIMULATING CONSCIENCE / Situational crime-prevention programs also have been developed to counteract the excuses and justifications used by offenders. After learning the linguistic devices that offenders use to make their crimes palatable to themselves, program designers can attack these belief systems. Such programs operate on the theory that, once their excuses have been neutralized, offenders will be less able to define their actions as acceptable, and thus have a harder time persisting with criminal behavior.[42] True to the roots of situational crime prevention, stimulating conscience in this way does not necessarily promote long-term changes in the prospective offender's personal dispositions, as do the cognitive-based programs used in correctional settings. Instead, situational crime-prevention theorists argue that programs geared toward removing excuses should focus on highly specific forms of crime and should be presented at the times criminal decisions are being made. The idea is to "stimulate feelings of conscience at the point of contemplating the commission of a specific kind of offense."[43] Theater ads that point out how piracy harms all who work on movie sets is an example of this idea in action.

Crime-reduction programs based on the premise of removing excuses have been developed for a number of different crimes. For example, researchers have found that excuses used to justify tax evasion can block the potentially inhibiting effects of guilt.[44] They suggest that campaigns designed to make tax cheaters feel guilty about their behaviors can reduce the prevalence of tax fraud. These principles also can be applied to identity theft. For this approach to work, however, it is necessary to present the appropriate message in the immediate context of the crime. While this might prove difficult for identity theft in general, a large proportion of such crimes are made possible by employees of businesses and agencies with legitimate access to personal identifying information. Clearly, dishonest employees play a role in the prevalence of identity theft. Thus, such interventions may be most effective when aimed at blocking excuses and justifications that allow illegal behavior to be committed within formal organizations, such as workplaces and schools.[45] A "remove excuses" campaign in workplaces also could serve to educate employees who might be tempted to misuse their positions to illegally sell sensitive information to others.[46] In any such campaign, organizational managers should openly discuss the neutralizations used by wayward employees. Introducing these neutralizations into the conversation will force employees to consciously consider their actions when they contemplate theft.[47]

ADVERTISING CONSEQUENCES / Identity thieves in our sample repeatedly voiced their expectations of lenient punishment—if they ever happened to be apprehended. This was one reason why so few seriously considered the risks of their crimes. The actual punishments that these offenders received, however, typically exceeded their expectations. Instead of probation or a few months of incarceration, as many thought, they received sentences ranging from one to thirty years. Their underestimates of the potential sentences contributed to their decisions to commit identity theft. It is therefore likely that educating potential thieves about the true consequences of arrest and conviction could persuade them to desist. It is always a difficult task to educate target populations about the costs of crime, but it is possible. Evidence shows that significant reductions in violence were achieved by implementing a "lever-pulling" strategy, involving face-to-face communication of a deterrence message.[48] Similar programs could be implemented to target both chronic identity thieves and the larger population.

Decades of deterrence research have shown that perceived punishments have a greater deterrent effect than actual punishments.[49] Thus, efforts to change the perceptions held by potential identity thieves should receive our initial attention. Campaigns designed to create the impression that law enforcement agencies consider identity theft to be a serious crime—and that such cases will be prosecuted to their fullest extent—could go a long way in changing offender perceptions. Although not all researchers agree on the value of publicity campaigns, such campaigns, if planned properly, may be cost-effective tools for preventing crime.[50]

WILL THIS REALLY WORK?

At a time when criminal justice policy aims to instill fear in the minds of offenders, particularly repeat offenders, we should recognize that the task is difficult, if not impossible, considering the ways in which persistent thieves think about the risks of their crimes. Programs and policies can be created to reduce the opportunities and increase the punishments associated with identity theft, but an offender's frame of mind may temper any deterrent potential of policies and practices that simply increase the risk and cost of crime. Due to misguided perceptions of their chances of being detected, or a mistaken belief that the punishments for their crimes will be negligible, some offenders remained undeterred by the possibility of formal sanctions. This is not to say that the weight of their actions carried no consequences for them. To the contrary, most were cognizant of the informal damages their actions caused, both to their personal relationships and to their own mental health. It appears, then, that the only consequences that some interviewees truly considered were these informal ones, although these too were slow-acting and insufficient deterrents.

One of the many challenges of crafting effective crime-prevention programs is anticipating how those prone to criminal behavior might adapt to the changing patterns of daily life. Like the rest of us, offenders have the human ability to recognize that, as one door closes, others open. They see opportunities for new crimes (or new methods for old crimes) where ordinary people may not. Thus, policies that focus exclusively on trying to deter the motivated offender through punishment or threats of punishment may not prove effective for reducing identity theft. The strategies most likely to be effective—at least until law enforcement and other security professionals catch up to identity thieves' ever-changing methods—are those exercised by victims and potential victims. We must be vigilant about protecting our personal information and monitoring our financial accounts. When people are victimized, it is vital that they immediately report the theft of their information to all the appropriate authorities, including the local police, the Federal Trade Commission, credit card companies, and other financial institutions. Despite crime-prevention programs that succeed in reducing the pool of potential identity thieves, there will continue to be a ready supply of motivated offenders. Potential victims—as well as law enforcement—should challenge themselves to continue to improve the protection of their personal information, and to deny thieves the opportunity to use that information if their protection fails.

One glimmer of hope in this discussion arises from the fact that more than half of offenders claimed that they wanted or planned to quit participating in fraud. The distancing of family and friends, the difficulties in maintaining secrets and lies, and the burden of guilt led many to consider giving up their larcenous ways. Overall, thirty-one in our sample of fifty-nine offenders (53 percent) stated that they wanted to get out of the stolen identity trade. Tameka, who claimed that she had already quit before she was arrested, said "I was tired. I was really tired. My sixteen-year-old daughter would be nervous, you know. I didn't know that they would be nervous when I flew. She was like, 'Mama I'm so tired, I mean I'm glad that you stopped 'cause we would be tired. I mean scared when you'd be gone that you wasn't gonna come back.'"

The stresses of hiding from the law, living day to day, managing drug addictions, and being without close others weighed heavily on the minds of many offenders. Fran claimed that, after each criminal venture, she would swear off crime. In her words, "After this I'm stopping. After this one I'm stopping. [But] it never did happen and there's no such thing as the next one going to be my last one. It's if you're going to stop, you're going to stop." (Fran reported that she came to this understanding only after spending time in rehabilitation classes, while in prison.) Jake claimed that the guilt associated with his actions began to increase as he continued his crimes, which fueled his desire to quit: "I got in the [criminal] group and once I felt it was going in the wrong direction I was trying to figure out how to get out, but I never did do it fast enough. What happened in my situation was the group had gotten involved in a case and they had an FBI sting involved where everybody got arrested. . . . I didn't get out fast enough, so it was my fault."

It is hard to determine the strength of these desires to quit offending, since few of these thieves had desisted before their arrests. When explaining why they did not quit, offenders often pointed to pressure from others, or to fear about a future without the financial support of their crimes.[51] It should be noted that 25 percent perceived their eventual arrest as "a relief." Those who wanted to quit, but lacked the willpower or financial security to do so, viewed arrest as an opportunity to regain a sense of normalcy in their lives.[52] In response to the question about what it was like to be arrested, Jessica said, "In a way it's kind of a sad, sick thing because it was kind of like a relief. I was like finally this will be over with." Similarly, Ed answered, "Oh it was a relief. It was! It was over. I'm glad, you know. I didn't even put up trouble."

Some considered their arrests and convictions as a chance for them to get clean and sober. As Dale described, "I was kind of glad that I was arrested, because I knew that I would get some help 'cause being in a no-smoking jail one time stopped me from smoking. So, I feel that this second round gonna really stop me from smoking drugs." Heidi, who also considered her drug addiction to be beyond her control, claimed, "I was trying to get busted so that I knew that I would get help." In describing her emotions when she was finally arrested, she said, "I felt relieved. I was. I felt relieved." Others viewed arrest as a route to renewed contact with their family. When asked what it was like when she was arrested, Bridgette said, "It was over. What was going to be done was done. I didn't have to worry. I could go back and be with my family when it was over and everything would be taken care of." All of these comments suggest that criminal behavior has serious consequences, and that a criminal lifestyle is not as easy or free as some portrayals would make it appear—at least not in the long run.

Although many entertained the thought of giving up a life of crime, they reported lacking the willpower to do so. In these circumstances, the threat of punishment did little to persuade them to stop, especially when punishment was perceived to carry little weight or was thought to be a better alternative to their current life. Indeed, the enticements of identity theft were strong for many of these participants. Only when offenders recognize the lasting damage that a criminal career inflicts on themselves and families do they begin to avoid criminal companions and situations altogether. At this later point, the threshold of fear necessary to deter them from crime is small in comparison. Yet, it does appear that even the most willful identity thieves are not completely immune from the consequences of their actions. Determining how to magnify their reservations—and exploit moments when they know they are vulnerable—may offer the most effective hope for deterrence.

Research on criminal decision-making makes clear that state crime-control policies grounded in notions of deterrence take insufficient account of factors and conditions that affect the subjective assessments of risk and reward by persistent offenders. While identity thieves do engage in seemingly rational decisions, the process is bounded by their desired lifestyles, their excuses and justifications for their crimes, their levels of skill and professionalism, and their perceptions of the (in)effectiveness of law enforcement. Thus, when making the decision to steal identities, they often are not attuned to the nuances of threatened penalties. Although identity thieves commit crimes that are generally considered white-collar offenses, they share some characteristics of street-level property offenders, often making "hurried, almost haphazard, decisions to offend while in a state of emotional turmoil."[53] What we know about the way criminals make decisions suggests that we should be wary of crime-control proposals that promise significant reductions in crime by increasing threats of punishment and incarceration. We do not suggest that legal threats are without some deterrent effect, only that "tinkering with them on the assumption offenders are aware of and behaviorally sensitive to the changes is naive or even disingenuous."[54] Developing better theoretical understandings of crime and criminality—and finding effective ways to prevent specific crimes—are hard rows to hoe. But relying on the accounts of offenders may make these tasks a little easier.

METHODOLOGICAL
APPENDIX

Criminologists have a long history of interviewing those engaged in illegal behaviors to gain insights into the nature of crime and criminality. Ethnographic interviews allow offenders to explain their offenses and lifestyles from their own perspectives. This is important because those engaged in criminal activities are in the "unique position of being able to describe, in their own words, the motivations and causes of crime, the level and nature of crime calculus, and the perceived effectiveness of crime control activities in deterring crime."[1] When the voices of those engaged in illegal activity are coupled with the researchers' analyses, students and criminal justice professionals have a more realistic picture of the world of offenders.[2] The researcher's job is to notice patterns in what offenders have to say, then organize those patterns. This is not an easy task, and subjective decisions must be made throughout the process. Such subjectivity is the foundation for much of the criticism of ethnographic research. Thus, we think it is important to be transparent with our methodology, so that others can make their own decisions about the validity and reliability of our research and the conclusions we draw from it. Our discussion of the research design focuses on both the advantages and challenges of conducting research in federal prisons, and on the strategies we employed to gain compliance from participants and elicit honest and meaningful answers to our questions.

Few would deny that posing open-ended questions to offenders is important for a full understanding of crime and criminality. One difficult part of seeking the offender perspective is locating suitable participants. While there are many places ethnographers can recruit offenders (street corners, bars, shelters, rehabilitation meetings, jails, or prisons, for example), we sought out offenders who were serving time in federal correctional facilities. We made this decision for several reasons. A major factor in our decision centered on the complexity of defining identity theft. By narrowing our sample to those convicted at the federal level, we were able to achieve some degree of standardization as to the types of offenders we interviewed (though the sample still exhibited considerable diversity). Specifically, we chose to exclude cases of credit card fraud in which offenders stole only existing account numbers and not the personally identifying information of their victims.

Additionally, the nature of identity theft differs greatly from other street crimes. Many who engage in the activity are not part of a criminal subculture (though some are). Thus, using traditional means of locating hard-to-reach populations, such as snowball or respondent-driven sampling, is quite difficult for this group. For such samples to be representative, it is necessary to tap into as many social networks as possible. While this approach might have produced a sample of street-level identity thieves, it likely would have failed to recruit the various types of offenders that represent the inherent diversity in this crime: members of occupational teams, street level identity thieves, and loners.

When seeking the perspectives of inmates, researchers face challenges that those interviewing active offenders do not, including skepticism from others about the validity of their findings.[3] Those who criticize the use of incarcerated-offender samples sometimes repeat the analogy of the animal in the zoo, to make the point that one cannot learn as much about crime and criminality from the incarcerated as one can from speaking to those in "the wild."[4] According to one proponent of active-offender samples, "We can no longer afford the convenient fiction that in studying criminals in their natural habitat, we would discover nothing really important that could not be discovered from criminals behind bars. What is true for studying the gorilla of zoology is likely to be even truer for studying the gorilla of criminology."[5] While this colorful metaphor has been often repeated, it may be specious. Non-human

animals do not have the ability to articulate their thoughts, decision processes, or motives, in the present or the past. Biologists
must observe animals in the wild because beasts cannot verbally
describe how and why they select certain prey, or otherwise interpret their actions to us.[6] Fortunately for social scientists, "our
subjects, unlike chemicals or cells or apes, are perfectly capable
of communicating to researchers, explaining what they have been
through, what they do, and what they hope to achieve with various
behaviours."[7] Because it is clearly unethical to accompany offenders while they commit identity theft, we thought it best to rely on
accounts of their thoughts and behaviors.

Additionally, there is no empirical evidence that active offenders
reveal different aspects about their lives and crimes than do incarcerated ones.[8] In fact, the limited amount of research comparing
the two types of samples shows consistency in the information
they provide.[9] And, even if accounts do differ between active and
incarcerated offenders, it is still not known which is more accurate
or rich for qualitative analysis. The lack of empirical validation for
the superiority of active-offender research means criminologists
risk repeating unsubstantiated conclusions drawn from secondary
sources solely because they seem to make sense. At present, we find
no convincing reason to conclude that the strategy of interviewing
incarcerated offenders about their crimes should be discarded.

In a similar vein, people often question whether offenders are
telling the truth about their crimes—or anything else, for that
matter—when being interviewed. We believe that the offenders
we spoke with responded to our questions truthfully, at least as
they saw the truth. We base this claim on several factors, including
the willingness of inmates to consent to interviews, particularly in
light of the fact that we were unable to offer any material benefits.
Federal Bureau of Prisons guidelines dictate that inmates cannot
receive monetary compensation for their participation. Granted,
we did offer a break from the daily routine of prison life, along with
new people to talk to, but money would undoubtedly have been
more persuasive.

In addition, we employed a style of interview that lessened the chance that offenders would lie. Simply put, they had no motiva-tion to lie about their backgrounds or their thoughts about com-mitting their crimes. Although they may have exaggerated or downplayed certain elements, such as the amount of money made on a particular theft or the frequency with which they committed their crimes, these "lies" pose no material threat to the validity of our understandings about their motivations, their assessments of the risks and rewards, their organizational patterns, or other as-pects of their offenses.[10]

SAMPLING STRATEGY

Using the reasons given previously as our foundation for adopt-ing a prison-based sample, we employed a purposive sampling strategy.[11] To locate federally convicted identity thieves, we relied primarily on three different types of sources: newspapers, legal documents, and press releases from U.S. attorneys' offices. Using the search term "identity theft" and specifying "all available years" in the LexisNexis search engine, we examined newspaper articles from each state to locate individuals who committed identity theft. The broadness of the search term resulted in many false hits, but through trial and error we concluded that this was the best strategy to ensure maximum inclusion of articles. In addition, we searched the LexisNexis Legal Research database, which contains decisions for federal courts, along with the Westlaw database, using the fed-eral statute for identity theft (18 U.S.C. § 1028). Finally, we searched the official Web site for U.S. attorneys, and the Web site of each in-dividual U.S. attorney for the ninety-three U.S. districts, for press releases about persons charged with, indicted for, or sentenced to prison for identity theft.

Once we had generated a list of names from our search of newspaper articles and legal documents, we then looked for these individuals on the Federal Bureau of Prisons Inmate Locator, to determine if they resided in the federal prison system.[12] Our search yielded the names of 470 individuals who had been sentenced to federal prison. Of these individuals, 117 had been released, 297 were housed in federal prisons, and the remaining 56 individuals were classified as "In Transit" or "Not in BOP Custody."

Our budget constraints made it impractical to interview all of the available inmates; thus, we drew a sample of participants by selecting the facilities with the largest number of inmates on our list in each of the six regions defined by the Federal Bureau of Prisons (Western, North Central, South Central, North Eastern, Mid-Atlantic, and South Eastern), then solicited inmates incarcerated in these prisons. Because some of these facilities were located near other federal prisons that housed individuals on our list, we also went to these facilities to interview offenders. We visited a total of fourteen correctional facilities and interviewed sixty-five individuals incarcerated for identity theft. Six offenders claimed to be innocent of all charges. These individuals either denied taking part in or having knowledge of the identity theft (if they had codefendants). Thus, our findings are based on the fifty-nine interviews in which participants acknowledged culpability for the crimes.

DATA COLLECTION

We used ethnographic interviews to explore offenders' life circumstances at the times of their crimes, their reasons for becoming involved in and continuing with identity theft, and the techniques they used to secure information to commit fraud and convert that information into cash or goods. Our goal was to have the participants tell their stories in their own words. Although we tried to ask the same questions of all participants, this was not always possible or appropriate. For example, questions about entering banks to cash checks were not applicable to those who engaged in mortgage fraud. Also, many participants began describing the events of their thefts even before we asked. On several occasions, participants described how they became involved in their crimes before we could ask all background questions. In these cases, we either tried to ask these questions at the end of the interview, or left them out. We did so because we did not want to disrupt the flow of conversation about the details of their thefts and their perceptions of their crimes, aspects of the interviews we deemed more important than background characteristics.

This style of interviewing is advantageous when investigators choose not to identify significant themes that may arise from dialogue with participants before research begins.[13] When investigators suspect that their participants' thinking and categorical schemes may be unfamiliar, or when discovery hinges on understanding how participants interpret and narrate their lives and actions, loosely structured interviews are best. The lack of previous research on the lives and experiences of identity thieves made this style of interview necessary. One downside of this style of interviewing is that not everyone is asked the same questions; thus, it is not always possible to generate frequency distributions of characteristics of thefts and thieves with the same number of participants.

When we approached inmates about participating, we explained what we were doing and how we selected them. As evidence of our sampling strategy, we gave potential participants a copy of the newspaper story we used to locate them. Doing so proved useful for several reasons. First, many were suspicious about why they were chosen to be interviewed. The newspaper story verified our approach. Moreover, by showing participants evidence that we had located them through a form of public media, we were able to relieve some of their suspicions that we were working on behalf of law enforcement or prison officials.[14] The story often acted as a launching pad for questions. Many claimed that the newspaper got it wrong; they were eager to "set the record straight" and share their version of events. This was particularly useful for those who were portrayed in a negative light—because they were identified as the ringleader, had profited excessively, or had purposely selected a particular type of victim (Jake, for example, was accused of targeting an elderly blind man but claimed that he did not know his victims). Although none of the interviewees (excluding the six exceptions noted previously) denied their participation in identity theft, many disputed at least some of the details reported in the newspaper.

Although researchers often pay participants cash stipends or offer them other forms of compensation, Federal Bureau of Prisons rules and regulations prohibit such transactions. Consequently, we were unable to offer participants money, food, beverages, or any other form of compensation for consenting to our interviews. We explained these rules to the inmates and suggested that the only "benefits" they might receive from their consenting would be time out of their cells, a break from their daily routines, and a chance to tell their side of the story. With the possible exception of one inmate who, while declining to be interviewed seemed to imply that there was nothing in it for him, our inability to offer inmates cash or goods did not seem to affect their decisions. Those who declined to be interviewed typically did so immediately after we introduced ourselves and told them why we wanted to speak with them.

We conducted the interviews from February 2006 to March 2007. Each interview lasted between forty-five minutes and two hours, with the majority of interviews lasting about one hour. Since the interviews were conducted over a thirteen-month period, interviews that took place later in the research were typically shorter and more focused. This was due in part to our practice of discussing the participants' responses and our interpretations immediately following the interviews. At the beginning, our study was largely exploratory; we simply did not have enough information about identity thieves to structure the interviews. As themes emerged, we were better able to focus our questions on particular issues. We learned to frame questions in ways that made sense to those we interviewed and to abandon lines of inquiry that were unproductive.

The interviews took place in private rooms in the prison facilities, such as private offices, visiting rooms, or attorney-client rooms. The one constant in the interview settings was that we were alone with participants during the interviews. While correctional officers were nearby, they were unable to listen to the conversations. This was important to our research, because we wanted participants to speak freely, without worrying that prison staff would overhear the details of their lives and crimes. When possible, we recorded interviews, then transcribed the audio verbatim.[15] However, some wardens denied us permission to bring recording devices into their facilities, and some offenders agreed to the interview only if it was not recorded. In addition, a few participants appeared hesitant to be recorded during the interview. We decided not to record these interviews to facilitate open conversation. Only eight of fifty-nine interviews were not recorded.

Both of us were present for the majority of the interviews, with one researcher acting as the lead interviewer, while the other took notes and ensured that important questions were not left out. While mixed-gendered, paired interviews are not the norm in qualitative research, we do think that this strategy was beneficial. First, it allowed one person to take more detailed notes during the interview; if questions were overlooked or new themes developed, this person could address them before the interview ended. This was especially important for those interviews where we were not granted permission to make a recording. With a second person taking notes, the lead interviewer could devote more attention to listening actively to the participant.

Perhaps more importantly, this style of interviewing facilitated rapport and encouraged a more relaxed atmosphere (at least from our perspective). Whereas the majority of participants directed their responses to both interviewers, alternating eye contact during responses, we noticed that several participants would interact with only one of us. When this happened, the interviewer being addressed would take the lead, even if this meant modifying the initial plan. Such incidences were typically directed along gender lines. Some male participants preferred to speak with the male interviewer (Heith), while some females preferred directing their responses to the female interviewer (Lynne).

Gender certainly has an impact on interviews, but not in a straightforward way.[16] Gender affects the stories that are relayed and the manner in which they are presented. As such, it is important to be sensitive to gender when conducting and analyzing interviews. We think that a mixed-gendered pairing worked to our advantage on several occasions. For example, a male participant, who seemed reluctant to participate at first, changed his mind after observing Lynne. He agreed to the interview saying, "I see you have come all this way and you're pregnant." On another occasion, a male participant from Eastern Europe was very reserved in his responses until Lynne took over the interview. After the interview, we asked why he had been more forthcoming with Lynne. In his home country, he said, etiquette dictated that he always honor the request of a pregnant woman.[17] While we always entered an interview with a plan for who would lead, we were flexible in changing these plans to facilitate rapport and stimulate responses. Although there are few specific protocols for conducting interviews, most researchers agree that being flexible and adjusting to the situation is vital to eliciting quality data from participants.

Additionally, paired interviewing guarded against interviewer fatigue. Because we were dependent on prison administrators to schedule interviews, we typically had to conduct multiple interviews on a single day. Practical experience suggests that conducting more than two interviews per day can lead to fatigue, increasing the risk of overlooking inconsistencies or of failing to ask sufficiently probing questions. By working as a team, we were able to forestall fatigue and maintain the quality of the interviews.

A final benefit of the paired structure was that it allowed us to discuss, process, and interpret participants' responses immediately following the interviews. We talked about what we "heard" and how it fit into our theoretical constructs. This process is consistent with grounded theory, a type of inductive theory in which observations are used to formulate a theory to explain those observations.[18] Thus, we could critically evaluate each other's interpretation of the interview while the participant's words were still fresh in our ears. Our shared travel allowed additional opportunities to discuss the interviews while sitting in hotel lobbies, driving to our destinations, and waiting in airports and on planes. As a result, we engaged in analysis throughout the data collection.

LIMITATIONS OF PRISON RESEARCH

We should note that doing research in prisons has unique limitations.[19] As researchers, we remain at the mercy of each facility's administration. While those administrators who allowed us access were very helpful, prison life is often unsuited for conducting research. Inmate counts and prison lockdowns sometimes delayed or prevented our ability to interview participants. Our first interview session was delayed for several hours because heavy fog prevented correctional officers from completing their daily census. On another occasion, our interviews were cancelled because an inmate was severely injured and the warden, fearing a race riot, initiated a total lockdown of the prison. Needless to say, we were asked to come back another day. On another trip we were blocked from even entering a facility because of a particularly tragic event. Federal agents had come to the facility to arrest several correctional officers for alleged indiscretions with inmates. Instead of surrendering, one officer, who had smuggled a firearm into the facility, engaged in a shootout that led to his own death and the death of a federal agent.

The primary limitation of our study, however, was related not to the administration of these prisons, but to their particular populations. Any sample based on convicted offenders may actually tell us more about enforcement patterns and priorities than about the actual distribution of crime.[20] We relied exclusively on interviews with federally convicted thieves to create our portrait of offenders, and it is possible that those convicted at the federal level are not representative of identity thieves in general. Jurisdictional issues often make the local prosecution of identity thieves difficult, if not legally impossible. For example, an offender who resides in Texas may steal the identity of a victim who lives in Louisiana and use that information to open credit card accounts at a department store in the offender's home state. Such cases—along with even more complicated cases, as well as those that involve multiple offenders—may be passed to federal authorities. In other situations, local prosecutors may not have the resources needed to prosecute offenders. Several offenders we spoke with suggested that local law enforcement agencies weren't equipped to handle their cases and simply chose to pass them along to federal officials. Others claimed that only the victim's persistence—after local officials refused to pursue the case—led to federal charges.[21] Additionally, federally convicted thieves may have been responsible for unusually high monetary losses or have had clear evidence against them, making prosecution easier. In our sample, however, the self-reported financial gains of those interviewed are comparable to reports from other researchers.[22]

ETHICS OF INTERVIEWING INMATES

When interviewing inmates, it is important to ensure that they are neither coerced into participating nor exposed to any undue harm by relaying information about crimes for which they have not been convicted. The potential exists that they may feel coerced into participating, either from excessive prodding by researchers or prison staff, or in the mistaken belief that they will accrue legal benefits (such as parole considerations) for consenting to participate. As Richard Wright and Scott Decker point out, "No matter how much inmates are assured otherwise, many will continue to believe what they say to researchers will get back to the authorities and influence their chances for early release."[23] We disagree with this position. Most inmates have enough experience, both personal and vicarious, with how the system works to know that their participation in research will have little impact on the parole board. In a separate project, we asked inmates if they thought speaking with us would help their chances of parole. One inmate replied:

> No. I'd like to say hell no. Shoot, if you can come to prison and do well for five or six years, build up a stack of certificates, try to do the right things and respect people, and try to change the way you use to be and go in front of the parole board and they still deny you for no apparent reason other than them just looking at your jacket and making their own opinion about you, then I don't see why this would help.

Of the forty inmates who were asked this question, not one thought they would receive any direct benefits with regard to parole.

Nevertheless, we thought it important to do our best to alleviate participants' perceived risk. To address the possibility of coercion or harm, we assured them of our confidentiality and reminded them that we could not help their position in the prison or their case for release in any way. We also included such statements in the consent form given to all participants. No inmates mentioned that they thought participation would help them with their legal status, as all had become familiar with prison bureaucracies and understand our lack of institutional clout. We also warned offenders not to reveal information so specific that it could help a prosecutor, which alleviated many fears about our motives as interviewers. In addition, we guaranteed that we would take all possible measures to keep their responses private. If prison staff did enter the interview room, which happened only a few times, we stopped asking questions until they left. Finally, before entering the prison we received assurances from prison administrators that they would not ask for any information elicited during the interviews.

It is also important to be wary of coercion to participate from prison staff. While we were not privy to any conversations that took place between participants and staff, those we interviewed made no mention of being pressured to do the interview. In addition, we received no complaints of any kind from inmates. We did, however, receive six letters from participants asking us to share the results of our study, which we have.

NOTES

INTRODUCTION

1. Mullins (2008, May 19).

2. For more on how thieves obtain information from others, see Gordon et al. (2007).

3. Javelin (2010).

4. See Gordon et al. (2007); Morris (2010); Rebovich (2009).

5. Synovate (2007); Javelin (2010).

6. Morris and Longmire (2008).

7. The specific code that prohibits the theft and unlawful use of personally identifying information is 18 U.S.C. § 1028(a)(7).

8. See 18 U.S.C. § 1028(a)(1)-(6) for the original code.

9. Hoar (2001).

10. Specifics about this can be found in 18 U.S.C. § 1028(a)(7).

11. For more information about the identity theft victimization survey, see Bureau of Justice Statistics (2006:2).

12. This definition comes from the President's Identity Theft Task Force (2007:2).

13. All names that appear in the text are aliases assigned by the authors.

14. For more on the definitional distinctions between identity theft and identity fraud, see Koops and Leenes (2006).

15. See Copes, Kerley, Kane, and Huff (2010) for discussion of the issue of including existing credit card fraud as a type of identity theft.

16. See Gordon et al. (2007) for offender data from U.S. Secret Service files and Allison, Schuck, and Lersch (2005) for data from local police departments.

17. LifeLock, a private service that offers identity theft protection services to its subscribers, has been sued by Experian for fraud and false advertising. Experian claimed that LifeLock used false and misleading advertising and has placed false fraud alerts on behalf of its clients (Desmond 2008).

18. Duffin, Keats, and Gill (2006) interviewed five identity thieves. A number of biographical and autobiographical accounts also discuss identity theft, including Hastings and Marcus (2006), Stickley (2008), and Sullivan (2004).

19. Broken windows theory maintains that physical signs of disorder send the message to residents, including criminals, that no one cares about the area. In such an environment, potential offenders perceive that they can easily commit crime. If neighborhood residents don't care enough to keep the streets clean and repair broken windows, they are unlikely to exercise social control over themselves, including those involved in criminal behavior.

20. For more on this issue, see St. Jean (2007).

21. Rengert and Wasilchick (1989:1).

22. The Inmate Locator is available on the Federal Bureau of Prisons' Web site (http://www.bop.gov/iloc2/LocateInmate.jsp). It allows people to search for inmates by their first and last names or inmate number.

23. See, for example, Becker (1968) and Cornish and Clarke (1986).

24. Opp (1997).

25. Clarke and Felson (1993:5). See also Clarke (1997).

26. Clarke and Cornish (1985); Cornish and Clarke (1986); Shover and Honaker (1992).

27. See Clarke and Cornish (1985); Opp (1997); and Simon (1957, 1978).

28. Jacobs and Wright (1999); Shover (1996).

29. Jacobs and Wright (1999:163).

30. Wright and Decker (1997).

31. Cromwell and Olson (2004).

32. Cornish (1994).

33. Newman (1997).

34. Clarke (1983, 1995).

1. PROFILES

1. Compiled from *New York Daily News* (http://www.nydailynews.com), August 17 and 19, 2009; and *U.S. v. Albert Gonzalez* at http://www.justice.gov/usao.com.

2. *Dallas Morning News*, February 5, 2010.

3. *New York Daily News*, January 18, 2011; U.S. Southern District of New York press release, available at http://www.justice.gov/usao/nys/pressreleases/January11/toneyadriennearrestpr.pdf.

4. See, for example, Allison et al. (2005), Gordon et al. (2007), Morris (2010), and Rebovich (2009).

5. Sixty-three percent of the offenders in Allison et al. (2005) were female, while in Gordon et al. (2007) and in Morris and Longmire (2008), the majority of offenders was male. Of the full list of identity thieves we located for our study, 63 percent were male.

6. See Rebovich (2009), who used data collected by Gordon et al. from U.S. Secret Service closed case files and by Copes and Vieraitis (2009b) in their interviews with offenders.

7. Morris (2010).

8. As explained in the appendix, we were unable to ask every interviewee all of these questions.

9. Much of this information comes from Copes and Vieraitis (2009b).

10. The full list of located inmates was 50 percent white, 46 percent black, and 4 percent other.

11. Information on the educational status of the interviewee was missing from nine interviews (15 percent of the sample).

12. Check kiting is defined as "the process in which cash is recorded in more than one bank account, but in reality the cash is either nonexistent or is in transit. Kiting schemes can be perpetrated using one bank and more than one account or between several banks and different accounts" (Association of Certified Fraud Examiners).

2. WHY THEY STEAL

1. For more on the motivations of offenders, see Shover (1996); Shover, Coffey, and Hobbs (2003); Wright and Decker (1994).

2. Bureau of Justice Statistics (2006).

3. Newman (2004).

4. The limited number of people mentioning these motivations for their crimes may be due to our sampling criteria rather than a true reflection of its frequency. It is unlikely that those who steal identities to hide from law enforcement or to get services or utilities would be prosecuted and sentenced at the federal level, which was part of the sampling criteria for this study. This type of identity theft is under-researched and, unfortunately, we are unable to shed much light on it. See Perl (2003).

5. Jacobs and Wright (2010); Shover (1996); Wright and Decker (1994).

6. Jacobs and Wright (1999); Shover (1996).

7. Jacobs and Wright (1999).

8. For more on the lifestyles of offenders see Brookman, Mullins, Bennett, and Wright (2007); Cromwell and Olson (2004); Shover (1996); Shover and Honaker (1992); Wright and Decker (1994).

9. Shover (1996:100).

10. Their backgrounds and motivations for engaging in identity theft were similar to those reported by other white-collar offenders. See Weisburd, Wheeler, Waring, and Bode (1991).

11. Duffield and Grabosky (2001).

12. See Lemert (1953:306) for more on this idea.

13. Cressey (1953:75).

14. Weisburd, Wheeler, Waring, and Bode (1991).

15. Katz (1988).

16. Lawrence hired people to enter banks and cash fraudulent checks for him.

17. See Katz (1988) for more on how crime is a demonstration of personal competence.

18. See Maruna and Copes (2005) and Orbuch (1997) for review of this literature.

19. Scott and Lyman (1968).

20. Holt and Copes (2010).

21. In previous articles based on this data, we elaborated on the neutralization techniques identity thieves used to relieve guilt (see Copes and Vieraitis 2009a; Copes, Vieraitis, and Jochum 2007). While similar to accounts, neutralization theory does differ in several regards. Most notably neutralization theory assumes causal order and the theory of accounts does not. See Maruna and Copes (2005) for review of this literature.

22. It was common for those with whom we spoke to use multiple accounts when making sense of their actions. Here Kendra simultaneously denies the victim and the injury she caused.

23. Here Ellen's account also includes the appeal to higher loyalties.

24. See Sykes and Matza's (1957) concept of condemning the condemners.

25. A previous quote from Bruce suggested that he thought his victims would benefit from his crimes. This provides more background as to why he thought this way.

26. This quote also contains elements of the condemnation of the condemners neutralization.

27. This excuse is also similar to the metaphor of the ledger, where offenders claim that when balancing the good they have done with the bad they have caused, they will have done more good acts (Klockars 1974).

28. Note that here Daphne also uses the denial of criminal intent by claiming that she was tricked into helping those with felonious intentions.

29. Scott and Lyman (1968).

30. Klenowski, Copes, and Mullins (2011) found similar results in their study of the influence of gender on accounts for white-collar crime.

31. Scott and Lyman (1968:47).

32. Scott and Lyman (1968:48).

33. Scott and Lyman (1968).

34. Mills (1940:904).

35. Klenowski, Copes, and Mullins (2011).

36. Klenowski, Copes, and Mullins (2011); Jesilow, Pontell, and Geis (1993); Willott, Griffin, and Torrance (2001).

3. HOW THEY DO IT

1. For example, McCarthy (1996), Morselli, Tremblay, and McCarthy (2006), and Warr (2002).

2. Much of this research began with Sutherland's (1937) classic work on the social organization of professional theft.

3. Akers (1998) and Sutherland (1937, 1947).

4. See Cressey (1953) for a discussion of embezzlers and Lemert (1958) for a discussion of check forgers.

5. For more on the social organization of burglars, motor vehicles thieves, and robbers, see Mullins and Cherbonneau (2011), Schneider (2005), and Wright and Decker (1994, 1997).

6. Pavlicek (2005).

7. Data from the National Crime Victimization Survey (BJS 2010) shows that many victims believed their information had been appropriated by family or friends. Readers should use caution when interpreting these statistics, since they are based on cases in which victims knew how their personal information had been stolen. In many identity theft cases, victims do not know how their information was stolen.

8. See Allison, Schuck, and Lersch (2005) and Kresse, Watland, and Lucki (2007).

9. Javelin Research and Strategy Group (2005).

10. Keith primarily worked alone, although he did have an accomplice in Mexico, who would cross the border to pick up Medicare checks and mail them to an account in the United Kingdom.

11. Best and Luckenbill (1994).

12. In this way they were similar to those embezzlers interviewed by Cressey (1953).

13. Recent research on gender and crime supports this finding that women are often blocked from participating in criminal networks (Miller and Mullins 2006; Mullins and Wright 2003).

14. This term was used by Cressey (1953) in describing the motivations of embezzlers.

15. While we briefly mention how and why thieves became initiated into identity theft here, a full description of motives can be found in chapter 2.

16. Celine reported that she was pressured by her husband to engage in this fraud. Although she knew of his involvement and benefited from the proceeds, she claimed to be unaware of all the details.

17. Best and Luckenbill (1994:44).

18. This characterization is similar to Best and Luckenbill's description of teams and the distinction they make with formal organizations.

19. Pavlicek (2005:30).

20. The roles developed by Pavlicek are generally consistent with the roles identified by the identity thieves from both occupational teams and SLIT rings in our sample.

21. In his discussion of SLIT ring members, Pavlicek includes the "victim identity source" and the "mule." Both serve as sources of the victim's identifying information but the victim identity source is an employee at a legitimate business while the mule is a street offender who gains this information as the result of his or her street crimes.

22. Pavlicek (2005).

23. A Beacon score is a ranking used to determine an individual's creditworthiness. The score helps determine interest rates for loans.

24. Best and Luckenbill (1994).

25. Best and Luckenbill (1994).

4. HOW THEY REDUCE RISK

1. Nee and Taylor (2000); Shover and Honaker (1992).

2. Wright and Decker (1994).

3. Cromwell and Olson (2004), Rengert and Wasilchick (2000); Wright (2001)

4. Shover and Honaker (1992).

5. See Rosoff, Pontell, and Tillman (2007) for a discussion of this idea.

6. For more on sentencing white collar offenders, see Friedrichs (2010).

7. For more on the use of such phrases by offenders, see Hochstetler and Copes (2006) and Walters (1990).

8. For research that examines arrest avoidance strategies of offenders, see Beauregard and Bouchard (2010); Cherbonneau and Copes (2006); Jacobs (1996a, 1996b); Johnson and Natarajan (1995).

9. Jacobs (1999).

10. Cherbonneau and Copes (2006).

11. Holt, Blevins, and Kuhns (2009).

12. For more on the targeting of robbery victims, see Brookman et al. (2007); Jacobs (2000); Lejeune (1977); Luckenbill (1980, 1981); Wright and Decker (1997).

13. Goffman (1971:257).

14. Steffensmeier and Ulmer (2005:128).

15. Copes, Forsyth, and Brunson (2007).

16. Steffensmeier and Ulmer (2005:128).

17. Steffensmeier (1986:190).

18. Faupel (1986); Maurer (1951); Sutherland (1937).

19. Lemert (1953).
20. Maurer (1940:186).

5. THEORETICAL AND POLICY IMPLICATIONS

1. Blumstein and Wallman (2000); Levitt (2004).
2. Topalli and Wright (forthcoming).
3. National White Collar Crime Center (2009).
4. Javelin Strategy and Research (2010).
5. Federal Trade Commission (2009).
6. Unisys (2009).
7. Piquero, Cohen, and Piquero (2011).
8. Higgins et al. (2010).
9. Javelin Strategy and Research (2009).
10. Lieber (2009).
11. Fetterman (2009).
12. Weaver and Carroll (1985); Feeney (1986); Topalli (2005).
13. See, for example, Blumstein, Cohen, and Farrington (1988) and Sampson and Laub (1993).
14. See Clarke and Cornish (1985) and Cornish and Clarke (1986).
15. See Blokland and Nieuwbeerta (2005), Greenberg (1991), Laub and Sampson (2003), and Piquero, Farrington, and Blumstein (2007).
16. See Bersani, Laub, and Nieuwbeerta (2009).
17. See Steffensmeier and Ulmer (2005) for a discussion of the factors that contribute to the careers of property offenders.
18. Cusson (1993); Paternoster et al. (1982).
19. Lejeune (1977).
20. Bennett and Wright (1984); Gill (2000).
21. Maruna and Copes (2005).
22. See Cromwell and Thurman (2003).
23. Hirschi (1969:208).
24. Akers (1985:60).
25. See, for example, Bennett and Wright (1984); Cromwell and Olson (2004); Jacobs and Wright (1999); Shover (1996); Wright and Decker (1994).
26. Jacobs and Wright (1999); Shover (1996).
27. Jacobs (1993, 1996a, 1996b); Jacobs and Miller (1998); Gibbs (1975).
28. Gibbs (1975:33).
29. Gibbs (1975:33).
30. Decker (2005); Rengert and Wasilchick (1989).
31. Clarke (1983, 1997).
32. Clarke (1997).
33. Berg (2009); Newman (2009); Willison (2009).
34. Newman and McNally (2005).
35. Newman and McNally (2005).
36. Newman (2009).
37. Newman (2004).
38. Clarke (1983).
39. Clarke (1983:246).

40. Hoofnagle (2007).

41. Hoofnagle (2007).

42. Clarke (1997); Clarke and Homel (1997)

43. Clarke (1997:24).

44. Thurman, St. John, and Riggs (1984).

45. Greenberg (1990); Lim (2002); Pelfrey (1984).

46. Lim (2002); Pelfrey (1984).

47. Cressey (1953).

48. Kennedy (1998); McGarrell et al. (2006).

49. Wright et al. (2004).

50. Johnson and Bowers (2003:497); for review see Mazerolle (2003).

51. The reasons they gave for not quitting were remarkably similar to the excuses and justifications given for their motivations for beginning their criminal careers.

52. See Shover and Copes (2010) for more detail on the feeling of relief when arrested.

53. Wright and Decker (1994:211).

54. Shover and Copes (2010:146).

METHODOLOGICAL APPENDIX

1. Miethe and McCorkle (2001:17).

2. Pogrebin (2004).

3. Copes and Hochstetler (2010).

4. See, for example, Jacques and Wright (2008).

5. Polsky (1998:116).

6. Despite Polsky's claim, primatologists have learned a considerable amount about primate behavior from studying captive animals, including how chimpanzees establish and maintain power dynamics within the group (de Waal 1980).

7. Maruna (2006:274).

8. Copes and Hochstetler (2010).

9. Nee (2003).

10. Sandberg (2010).

11. We borrowed from the work of Shover, Coffey, and Sanders (2004) in determining how to locate these offenders.

12. The "Inmate Locator" is available on the Federal Bureau of Prisons' Web site (http://www.bop.gov/iloc2/LocateInmate.jsp). It allows people to search for inmates by their first and last names or inmate number.

13. See Spradley (1979) for more on ethnographic interviewing.

14. Several noted that they initially were hesitant to speak with us, as they feared we might have been working for the FBI or other law enforcement agency. All acknowledged after meeting with us that this concern had been alleviated.

15. During transcription, we removed all identifying remarks. In addition, we assigned an alias to each participant.

16. Miller (2010).

17. We recognize that some readers may question whether we coerced him into participating in the interview. However, we were unaware of this belief system until after the interview had been completed, and asked no further questions about his crimes after he revealed this custom.

18. For more on grounded theory, see Glaser and Strauss (1967).

19. Schlosser (2008).

20. Jesilow, Pontell, and Geis (1993).

21. For more on the difficulties of determining jurisdiction for prosecuting identity theft, see White and Fisher (2008).

22. See, for example, Bureau of Justice Statistics (2007), Federal Trade Commission (2004), and Gordon et al. (2007).

23. Wright and Decker (1997:4).

BIBLIOGRAPHY

Akers, Ronald L. 1985. *Deviant Behavior: A Social Learning Approach.* Third ed. Belmont, CA: Wadsworth.

Akers, Ronald L. 1998. *Social Learning and Social Structure: A General Theory of Crime and Deviance.* Boston: Northeastern University Press.

Allison, Stuart, Amie Schuck, and Kim M. Lersch. 2005. "Exploring the Crime of Identity Theft: Prevalence, Clearance Rates, and Victim/Offender Characteristics." *Journal of Criminal Justice* 33:19–29.

Beauregard, Eric, and Martin Bouchard. 2010. "Cleaning Up Your Act: Forensic Awareness as a Detection Avoidance Strategy." *Journal of Criminal Justice* 38:1160–1166.

Becker, Gary S. 1968. "Crime and Punishment: An Economic Approach." *Journal of Political Economy* 76:169–217.

Bennett, Trevor, and Richard Wright. 1984. *Burglars on Burglary: Prevention and the Offender.* Aldershot: Gower.

Berg, Sara. 2009. "Preventing Identity Theft through Information Technology." In *Perspectives on Identity Theft,* edited by M. McNally and G. Newman, 151–168. Crime Prevention Studies 23. Monsey, NY: Criminal Justice Press.

Bersani, Bianca, John H. Laub, and Paul Nieuwbeerta. 2009. "Marriage and Desistance for Crime in the Netherlands: Do Gender and Socio-Historical Context Matter." *Journal of Quantitative Criminology* 25:3–24.

Best, Joel, and David Luckenbill. 1994. *Organizing Deviance.* Second ed. Upper Saddle River, NJ: Prentice Hall.

Blokland, Arjan, and Paul Nieuwbeerta. 2005. "The Effects of Life Circumstances on Longitudinal Trajectories of Offending." *Criminology* 43:1203–1240.

Blumstein, Alfred, Jacqueline Cohen, and David Farrington. 1988. "Criminal Career Research: Its Value for Criminology." *Criminology* 26:1–35.

Blumstein, Alfred, and Joel Wallman. 2000. *The Crime Drop in America.* New York: Cambridge University Press.

Brookman, Fiona, Christopher Mullins, Trevor Bennett, and Richard Wright. 2007. "Gender, Motivation and the Accomplishment of Street Robbery in the United Kingdom." *British Journal of Criminology* 47:861–884.

Bureau of Justice Statistics. 2006. *Identity Theft, 2004.* Washington, DC: U.S. Government Printing Office.

Bureau of Justice Statistics. 2007. *Identity Theft, 2005.* Washington, DC: U.S. Government Printing Office.

Bureau of Justice Statistics. 2010. *Identity Theft Reported by Households, 2007—Statistical Tables.* Washington, DC: U.S. Government Printing Office.

Cherbonneau, Michael, and Heith Copes. 2006. "Drive It Like You Stole It: Auto Thieves and the Illusion of Normalcy." *British Journal of Criminology* 46:193–211.

Clarke, Ronald V. 1983. "Situational Crime Prevention: Its Theoretical Basis and Practical Scope." In *Crime and Justice: An Annual Review of Research,* vol. 4, edited by M. Tonry and N. Morris, 225–256. Chicago: University of Chicago Press.

Clarke, Ronald V. 1995. "Situational Crime Prevention." In *Building a Safer Society: Strategic Approaches to Crime Prevention,* edited by M. Tonry and D. Farrington, 91–151. Chicago: University of Chicago Press.

Clarke, Ronald V., ed. 1997. *Situational Crime Prevention: Successful Case Studies.* Guilderland, NY: Harrow and Heston.

Clarke, Ronald V., and Derrick Cornish. 1985. "Modeling Offenders' Decisions: A Framework for Research and Policy." In *Crime and Justice,* vol. 6, edited by M. Tonry and N. Morris, 147–185. Chicago: University of Chicago Press.

Clarke, Ronald V., and Marcus Felson. 1993. "Introduction: Criminology, Routine Activity, and Rational Choice." In *Routine Activity and Rational Choice: Advances in Criminological Theory,* edited by R. V. Clarke and M. Felson, 1–16. New Brunswick, NJ: Transaction Publishers.

Clarke, Ronald V., and Ross Homel. 1997. "A Revised Classification of Situational Crime Prevention Techniques." In *Crime Prevention at a Crossroads,* edited by S. P. Lab, 21–35. Cincinnati: Anderson.

Copes, Heith, and Andy Hochstetler. 2010. "Interviewing the Incarcerated: Pitfalls and Promises." In *Offenders on Offending: Learning About Crime From Criminals,* edited by W. Bernasco, 49–67. Cullompton, Devon, UK: Willan Publishers.

Copes, Heith, Craig Forsyth, and Rod Brunson. 2007. "Rock Rentals: The Social Organization and Interpersonal Dynamics of Crack-for-Cars Transactions in Louisiana, USA." *British Journal of Criminology* 47:885–899.

Copes, Heith, Kent Kerley, John Kane, and Rodney Huff. 2010. "An Exploratory Study of Identity Theft Victims Using a National Victimization Survey." *Journal of Criminal Justice* 38:1045–1052.

Copes, Heith, and Lynne M. Vieraitis. 2009a. "Bounded Rationality of Identity Thieves: Using Offender-Based Research to Inform Policy." *Criminology and Public Policy* 8:237–262.

Copes, Heith, and Lynne M. Vieraitis. 2009b. "Understanding Identity Theft: Offenders' Accounts of Their Lives and Crimes." *Criminal Justice Review* 34:329–349.

Copes, Heith, Lynne M. Vieraitis, and Jen Jochum. 2007. "Bridging the Gap Between Research and Practice: How Neutralization Theory can Inform Reid Interrogations of Identity Thieves." *Journal of Criminal Justice Education* 18:444–459.

Cornish, Derek. 1994. "The Procedural Analysis of Offending and Its Relevance for Situational Prevention." In *Crime Prevention Studies,* vol. 3, edited by R. V. Clarke, 151–196. Monsey, NY: Criminal Justice Press.

Cornish, Derek, and Ronald V. Clarke, eds. 1986. *The Reasoning Criminal.* New York: Springer.

Cressey, Donald R. 1953. *Other People's Money: A Study in the Social Psychology of Embezzlement.* Glencoe, IL: Free Press.

Cromwell, Paul, and Avery Olson. 2004. *Breaking and Entering: Burglars on Burglary.* Belmont, CA: Wadsworth.

Cromwell, Paul, and Quint Thurman. 2003. "The Devil Made Me Do It: Use of Neutralizations by Shoplifters." *Deviant Behavior* 24:535–550.

Cusson, M. 1993. "Situational Deterrence: Fear During the Criminal Event." In *Crime Prevention Studies*, vol. 1, edited by R. Clarke, 55–68. Monsey, NY: Willow Tree Press.

de Waal, Frans. 1982. *Chimpanzee Politics: Power and Sex among Apes.* London: Jonathan Cape.

Decker, Scott. 2005. *Using Offender Interviews to Inform Police Problem Solving.* Problem-Oriented Guides for Police Problem-Solving Tools Series No. 3. Washington, DC: U.S. Department of Justice.

Desmond, Maurna. 2008. "Experian v. LifeLock: Fraud is in the Eye of the Beholder." Forbes.com. Retrieved June 16, 2010 (http://www.forbes.com/2008/02/21/experian-lifelock-lawsuit-markets-equity-cx_md_0221-markets17.html).

Duffield, Grace, and Peter Grabosky. 2001. *The Psychology of Fraud.* Trends and Issues in Crime and Criminal Justice No. 199. Canberra, Australia: Australian Institute of Criminology,

Duffin, Michelle, Gemma Keats, and Martin Gill. 2006. *Identity Theft in the UK: The Offender and Victim Perspective.* Leicester, UK: Perpetuity Research and Consultancy International.

Faupel, Charles E. 1986. "Heroin Use, Street Crime, and the 'Main Hustle': Implications for the Validity of Official Crime Data." *Deviant Behavior* 7:31–45.

Federal Trade Commission. 2004. "National and State Trends in Fraud and Identity Theft." January–December 2003. Retrieved February 2, 2011 (http://www.ftc.gov).

Federal Trade Commission. 2009. *Consumer Sentinel Network Data Book for January to December 2008.* Retrieved on February 2, 2011, (http://www.ftc.gov/sentinel/reports/sentinel-annual-reports/sentinel-cy2008.pdf).

Feeney, Floyd. 1986. "Robbers as Decision Makers." In *The Reasoning Criminal: Rational Choice Perspectives on Offending,* edited by D. Cornish and R. Clarke, 53–71. New York: Springer-Verlag.

Fetterman, Mindy. 2009. "Identity Theft, new law about to send shredding on a tear." *USA Today,* January 14, 2005. Retrieved on September 24, 2010 (http://www.usatoday.com/money/perfi/general/2005–01–14-shredder-cover_x.htm?loc=interstitialskip).

Friedrichs, David. 2010. *Trusted Criminals: White Collar Crime in Contemporary Society.* Fourth ed. New York: Wadsworth.

Gibbs, Jack. 1975. *Crime, Punishment, and Deterrence.* New York: Elsevier.

Gill, Martin. 2000. *Commercial Robbery.* London: Blackstone Press Limited.

Glaser, Barney, and Anselm Strauss. 1967. *The Discovery of Grounded Theory.* Chicago: University of Chicago Press.

Goffman, Erving. 1971. *Relations in Public: Micro Studies of the Public Order.* New York: Basic Books.

Gordon, Gary R., Donald Rebovich, Kyung-Seok Choo, and Judith B. Gordon. 2007. *Identity Fraud Trends and Patterns: Building a Data-Based Foundation for Proactive Enforcement.* Utica, NY: Center for Identity Management and Information Protection.

Greenberg, David F. 1991. "Modeling Criminal Careers." *Criminology* 29:17–45.

Greenberg, Jerald. 1990. "Employee Theft as a Reaction to Underpayment Inequity: The Hidden Cost of Pay Cuts." *Journal of Applied Psychology* 75:561–68.

Hastings, Glenn, and Richard Marcus. 2006. *Identity Theft, Inc.: A Wild Ride with the World's #1 Identity Thief.* New York: The Disinformation Company.

Higgins, George, Thomas Hughes, Melissa Ricketts, and Brian Fell. 2010. "Self-protective Identity Theft Behaviors of College Students: An Exploration Using the Rasch Person-Item Map." *Southwest Journal of Criminal Justice* 7:24–45.

Hirschi, Travis. 1969. *Causes of Delinquency.* Berkeley: University of California Press.

Hoar, Sean B. 2008. "Identity Theft: The Crime of the New Millennium." *Oregon Law Review* 80:1423–1442.

Hochstetler, Andy, and Heith Copes. 2006. "Managing Fear to Commit Felony Theft." In *In Their Own Words: Criminals on Crime,* fourth ed., edited by P. Cromwell, 102–112. Los Angeles, CA: Roxbury.

Holt, Thomas J., and Heith Copes. 2010. "Transferring Subcultural Knowledge Online: Practices and Beliefs of Persistent Digital Pirates." *Deviant Behavior* 31:625–654.

Holt, Thomas, Kristie Blevins, and Joseph Kuhns. 2009. "Examining Diffusion and Arrest Avoidance Practices among Johns." *Crime and Delinquency,* DOI: 10.1177/0011128709347087.

Hoofnagle, Jay. 2007. "Identity Theft: Making the Known Unknowns Known." *Harvard Journal of Law and Technology* 21:97–122.

Jacobs, Bruce. 1993. "Undercover Deception Clues: A Case of Restrictive Deterrence." *Criminology* 31:281–99.

Jacobs, Bruce. 1996a. "Crack Dealers and Restrictive Deterrence: Identifying Narcs." *Criminology* 34:409–31.

Jacobs, Bruce. 1996b. "Crack Dealers Apprehension Avoidance Techniques: A Case of Restrictive Deterrence." *Justice Quarterly* 13:359–81.

Jacobs, Bruce. 1999. *Dealing Crack: The Social World of Streetcorner Selling.* Boston, MA: Northeastern University Press.

Jacobs, Bruce. 2000. *Robbing Drug Dealers: Violence Beyond the Law.* New York: Aldine de Gruyter.

Jacobs, Bruce, and Jody Miller. 1998. "Crack Dealing, Gender, and Arrest Avoidance." *Social Problems* 45:550–69.

Jacobs, Bruce, and Richard Wright. 1999. "Stick-Up, Street Culture, and Offender Motivation." *Criminology* 37:149–73.

Jacobs, Bruce, and Richard Wright. 2010. "Bounded Rationality, retaliation, and the Spread of Urban Violence." *Journal of Interpersonal Violence* 25:1739–1766.

Jacques, Scott, and Richard Wright. 2008. "Intimacy with Outlaws: The Role of Relational Distance in Recruiting, Paying, and Interviewing Underworld Research Participants." *Journal of Research in Crime and Delinquency* 45:22–38.

Javelin Strategy and Research. 2005. *2005 Identity Fraud Survey Report.* Pleasanton, CA: Javelin Strategy and Research Group.

Javelin Strategy and Research. 2009. *2009 Identity Fraud Survey Report.* Pleasanton, CA: Javelin Strategy and Research Group.

Javelin Strategy and Research. 2010. *2010 Identity Fraud Survey Report: Consumer Version.* Pleasanton, CA: Javelin Strategy and Research Group.

Jesilow, Paul, Henry N. Pontell, and Gilbert Geis. 1993. *Prescription for Profit: How Doctors Defraud Medicaid.* Berkeley: University of California Press.

Johnson, Bruce, and Mangai Natarajan. 1995. "Strategies to Avoid Arrest: Crack Sellers' Response to Intensified Policing." *American Journal of Police* 14:49–69.

Johnson, Shane D., and Kate J. Bowers. 2003. "Opportunity is in the Eye of the Beholder: The Role of Publicity in Crime Prevention." *Criminology and Public Policy* 2:497–524.

Katz, Jack. 1988. *Seductions of Crime: Moral and Sensual Attractions of Doing Crime.* New York: Basic Books.

Kennedy, David. 1998. "Pulling Levers: Getting Deterrence Right." *National Institute of Justice Journal* 236:2–8.

Klenowski, Paul, Heith Copes, and Christopher Mullins. 2011. "Gender, Identity and Accounts: How White Collar Offenders Do Gender when They Make Sense of Their Crimes." *Justice Quarterly* 28:46–69.

Klockars, Carl B. 1974. *The Professional Fence.* New York: Macmillan.

Koops, Bert-Jaap, and Ronald Leenes. 2006. "Identity Theft, Identity Fraud and/ or Identity-related Crime." *Datenschutz und Datensicherheit* 30:553–556.

Kresse, William, Kathleen Watland, and John Lucki. 2007. *Identity Theft: Findings and Public Policy Recommendations.* Final report to the Institute for Fraud Prevention (http://www.sxu.edu/Academic/Graham/Documents/identity_ theft_study.pdf).

Laub, John H., and Robert J. Sampson. 2003. *Shared Beginnings, Divergent Lives: Delinquent Boys to Age 70.* Cambridge, MA: Harvard University Press.

Lejeune, R. 1977. "The Management of a Mugging." *Urban Life* 6:123–47.

Lemert, Edwin. 1953. "An Isolation and Closure Theory of Naive Check Forgery." *Journal of Criminal Law, Criminology, and Police Science* 44:296–307.

Lemert, Edwin. 1958. "The Behavior of the Systematic Check Forger." *Social Problems* 6:141–149.

Levitt, Steven D. 2004. "Understanding Why Crime Fell in the 1990s: Four Factors that Explain the Decline and Six that Do Not." *Journal of Economic Perspectives* 18:163–190.

Lieber, Ron. 2009. "Credit Monitoring Services Are a Waste of Money, Critics Say." *The News & Observer*, November 3. Retrieved March 12, 2010 (http:// www.newsobserver.com).

Lim, Vivien K. G. 2002. "The IT Way of Loafing on the Job: Cyberloafing, Neutralizing and Organizational Justice." *Journal of Organizational Behavior* 23:675–94.

Luckenbill, David F. 1980. "Patterns of Force in Robbery." *Deviant Behavior* 1:361–378.

Luckenbill, David F. 1981. "Generating Compliance: The Case of Robbery." *Urban Life* 10:26–46.

Maruna, Shadd. 2006. "Review of *In Their Own Words: Criminals on Crime.*" *Australian and New Zealand Journal of Criminology* 39:274–275.

Maruna, Shadd, and Heith Copes. 2005. "What We Have Learned from Five Decades of Neutralization Theory Research." *Crime and Justice: A Review of Research* 32:221–320.

Maurer, David W. 1940. *The Big Con.* Indianapolis: Bobbs-Merrill.

Maurer, David W. 1951. *Whiz Mob: A Correlation of the Technical Argot of Pickpockets with Their Behavior Patterns.* Gainesville, FL: American Dialect Society.

Mazerolle, Lorraine. 2003. "The Pros and Cons of Publicity Campaigns as a Crime Control Tactic." *Criminology and Public Policy* 2:531–540.

McCarthy, Bill. 1996. "The Attitudes and Actions of Others: Tutelage and Sutherland's Theory of Differential Association." *British Journal of Criminology* 36:135–147.

McGarrell, Edmund F., Steven Chermak, Jeremy M. Wilson, and Nicholas Corsaro. 2006. "Reducing Homicide Through a 'Lever-Pulling' Strategy." *Justice Quarterly* 23:214–231.

Meek, James Gordon, and Corky Siemaszko. 2009. "'Soupnazi' Hacker Albert Gonzalez Went from Nerdy Past to Life of Sex, Guns and Drugs." *New York Daily News,* August 18. Retrieved January 28, 2011 (http://www.nydailynews.com).

Miethe, Terance D., and Richard C. McCorkle. 2001. *Crime Profiles: The Anatomy of Dangerous Persons, Places and Situations.* Los Angeles, CA: Roxbury.

Miller, Jody. 2010. "The Impact of Gender when Interviewing Offenders on Offending." In *Offenders on Offending: Learning About Crime From Criminals,* edited by W. Bernasco, 161–183. Cullompton, Devon, UK: Willan Publishers.

Miller, Jody, and Chris Mullins. 2006. "The Status of Feminist Theories in Criminology." In *Taking Stock: The Status of Criminological Theory, Advances in Criminological Theory* 15, edited by F. T. Cullen, J. P. Wright, and K. R. Blevins, 217–249. New Brunswick, NJ: Transaction Publishers.

Mills, C. Wright. 1940. "Situated Actions and Vocabularies of Motive." *American Sociological Review* 5:904–13.

Morris, Robert G. 2010. "Identity Thieves and Sophistication Levels: Findings from a National Probability Sample of American Newspaper Articles." *Deviant Behavior* 31:184–207.

Morris, Robert G., and Dennis R. Longmire. 2008. "Media Constructions of Identity Theft." *Journal of Criminal Justice & Popular Culture* 15:1–17.

Morselli, Carlo, Pierre Tremblay, and Bill McCarthy. 2006. "Mentors and Criminal Achievement." *Criminology* 44:17–43.

Mullins, Chris W., and Michael Cherbonneau. 2011. "Establishing Connections: Gender, Motor Vehicle Theft, and Disposal Networks." *Justice Quarterly* 28:278–302.

Mullins, Chris W., and Richard Wright. 2003. "Gender, Social Networks, and Residential Burglary." *Criminology* 41:813–840.

Mullins, Luke. 2008. "How Frank Abagnale Would Swindle You." *US News & World Report,* May 19. Retrieved February 2, 2011 (http://money.usnews.com).

National White Collar Crime Center. 2009. *White Collar Crime Statistics (2009).* Fairmont, WV: National White Collar Crime Center.

Nee, Claire. 2003. "Burglary Research at the End of the Millennium: An Example of Grounded Theory?" *Security Journal* 16:37–44.

Nee, Claire, and Max Taylor. 2000. "Examining Burglars' Target Selection: Interview, Experiment, or Ethnomethodology?" *Psychology, Crime, and Law* 6:45–59.

Newman, Graeme. 1997. "Introduction: Towards a Theory of Situational Crime Prevention. In *Rational Choice and Situational Crime Prevention: Theoretical Foundations,* edited by G. Newman, R. Clarke, and G. Shoham, 1–23. Brookfield, VT: Dartmouth.

Newman, Graeme. 2004. *Identity Theft,* Problem-Oriented Guides for Police, Problem-Specific Guides Series No. 24. Washington, DC: U.S. Department of Justice.

Newman, Graeme. 2009. "Identity Theft and Opportunity." In *Perspectives on Identity Theft,* Crime Prevention Studies, vol. 23, edited by M. McNally and G. Newman, 9–32. Monsey, NY: Criminal Justice Press.

Newman, Graeme R., and Megan M. McNally. 2005. *Identity Theft Literature Review.* Washington DC: U.S. Department of Justice, National Institute of Justice.

Opp, Karl-Dieter. 1997. "Limited Rationality and Crime." In *Rational Choice and Situational Crime Prevention,* edited by G. Newman, R. V. Clarke, and S. G. Shoham, 52–75. Brookfield, VT: Dartmouth.

Orbuch, Terri L. 1997. "People's Accounts Count: The Sociology of Accounts." *Annual Review of Sociology* 23:455–478.

Paternoster, Raymond, Linda Saltzman, Ted Chiricos, and Gordon Waldo. 1982. "Perceived Risk and Deterrence: Methodological Artifacts in Perceptual Deterrence Research." *Journal of Criminal Law and Criminology* 73:1238–58.

Pavlicek, Bruno. 2005. "Identity Theft and SLIT Rings: An Unrecognized yet Growing Cancer." *Crime and Justice International* 21:29–33.

Pelfrey, William V. 1984. "Keep Honest Employees Honest." *Security Management* 6:22–24.

Perl, Michael. 2003. "It's Not Always about the Money: Why the State Identity Theft Laws Fail to Adequately Address Criminal Record Identity Theft." *Journal of Criminal Law and Criminology* 94:169–208.

Piquero, Alex R., David P. Farrington, and Alfred Blumstein. 2007. *Key Issues in Criminal Career Research: New Analyses of the Cambridge Study in Delinquent Development.* Cambridge: Cambridge University Press.

Piquero, Nicole, Mark A. Cohen, and Alex Piquero. 2011. "How Much is the Public Willing to Pay to be Protected from Identity Theft?" *Justice Quarterly* 28:437–459.

Pogrebin, Mark. 2004. *About Criminals: A View of the Offender's World.* Thousand Oaks, CA: Sage.

Polsky, Ned. 1998. *Hustlers, Beats and Others* (expanded edition). New York: Lyons Press.

President's Identity Theft Task Force. 2007. *Combating Identity Theft: A Strategic Plan.* Retrieved February 2, 2011 (http://www.idtheft.gov/reports/StrategicPlan.pdf).

Rebovich, Donald J. 2009. "Examining Identity Theft: Empirical Explorations of the Offense and the Offender." *Victims and Offenders* 4:357–364.

Rengert, George. F., and John Wasilchick. 1989. *Space, Time and Crime: Ethnographic Insights into Residential Burglary.* Final report submitted to the National Institute of Justice. Washington, DC: U.S. Department of Justice.

Rosoff, Stephen M., Henry Pontell, and Robert H. Tillman. 2007. *Profit Without Honor: White-collar Crime and the Looting of America,* fourth ed. Upper Saddle River, NJ: Prentice Hall.

Sampson, Robert J. and John H. Laub. 1993. *Crime in the Making: Pathways and Turning Points through Life.* Cambridge, MA: Harvard University Press.

Sandberg, Sveinung. 2010. "What Can 'Lies' Tell Us About Life? Notes Towards a Framework of Narrative Criminology." *Journal of Criminal Justice Education* 21:447–465.

Schifrel, Scott. 2011. "Parks and Recreation Employee Busted for ID Theft, Joins Four Others Nabbed for Similar Scheme." *New York Daily News,* January 18. Retrieved January 28, 2011 (http://www.nydailynews.com).

Schlosser, Jennifer. 2008. "Issues in Interviewing Inmates: Navigating the Methodological Landmines of Prison Research." *Qualitative Inquiry* 14:1500–1525.

Schneider, Jacqueline L. 2005. "Stolen Goods Market: Methods of Disposal." *British Journal of Criminology,* 45:129–140.

Scott, Marvin B., and Stanford Lyman. 1968. "Accounts." *American Sociological Review* 33:46–62.

Shover, Neal. 1996. *Great Pretenders: Pursuits and Careers of Persistent Thieves.* Boulder, CO: Westview.

Shover, Neal, Glenn Coffey, and Dick Hobbs. 2003. "Crime on the Line: Telemarketing and the Changing Nature of Professional Crime." *British Journal of Criminology* 43:489–505.

Shover, Neal, Glenn Coffey, and Clinton Sanders. 2004. "Dialing for Dollars: Opportunities, Justifications and Telemarketing Fraud." *Qualitative Sociology* 27:59–75.

Shover, Neal, and Heith Copes. 2010. "Decision Making by Persistent Thieves and Crime-Control Policy." In *Crime and Public Policy,* edited by H. Barlow and S. Decker, 128–149. Boulder, CO: Westview.

Shover, Neal, and David Honaker. 1992. "The Socially Bounded Decision Making of Persistent Property Offenders." *Howard Journal of Criminal Justice* 31:276–293.

Simon, Herbert. 1957. *Models of Man: Social and Rational.* New York: Wiley

Simon, Herbert. 1978. "Rationality as a Process and Product of Thought." *American Economic Review* 8:1–11.

Spradley, James. 1979. *The Ethnographic Interview.* New York: Rinehart and Winston.

St. Jean, Peter. 2007. *Pockets of Crime: Broken Windows, Collective Efficacy, and the Criminal Point of View.* Chicago: University of Chicago Press.

Steffensmeier, Darrell. 1986. *The Fence: In the Shadow of Two Worlds.* Lanham, MD: Rowan and Littlefield.

Steffensmeier, Darrell, and Jeffery Ulmer. 2005. *Confessions of a Dying Thief: Understanding Criminal Careers and Illegal Enterprises.* New Brunswick, NJ: Transaction.

Stickley, Jim. 2008. *The Truth about Identity Theft.* Upper Saddle River, NJ: FT Press.

Suddath, Claire. 2009. "Master Hacker Albert Gonzalez." *Time,* August 19. Retrieved January 28, 2011 (http://www.time.com).

Sullivan, Bob. 2004. *Your Evil Twin: Behind the Identity Theft Epidemic.* Hoboken, NJ: John Wiley and Sons.

Sutherland, Edwin H. 1937. *The Professional Thief.* Chicago: University of Chicago Press.

Sutherland, Edwin H. 1947. *Principles of Criminology,* fourth ed. Philadelphia: Lippincott.

Sykes, Gresham, and David Matza. 1957. "Techniques of Neutralization: A Theory of Delinquency." *American Sociological Review* 22:664–70.

Synovate. 2007. *Federal Trade Commission—2006 Identity Theft Survey Report* [online]. Retrieved February 2, 2011 (www.ftc.gov/os/2007/11/SynovateFinalReportIDTheft2006.pdf).

Thurman, Quint C., Craig St. John, and Lisa Riggs. 1984. "Neutralizations and Tax Evasion: How Effective Would a Moral Appeal be in Improving Compliance to Tax Laws?" *Law and Policy* 6:309–28.

Topalli, Volkan. 2005. "Criminal Expertise and Offender Decision-Making." *British Journal of Criminology* 45:269–295.

Topalli, Volkan, and Richard Wright. Forthcoming. "Choosing Street Crime." In *Oxford Handbook of Criminological Theory,* edited by Frank Cullen and Pamela Wilcox. New York: Oxford University Press.

Unisys. 2009. *Unisys Security Index Reveals High Concern among Americans about Government and Business Protection of Private Data.* Retrieved on January 20, 2010 (http://www.unisys.com).

Unmuth, Katherine Leal. 2010. "Woman Sentenced to 34 Years for Stealing Irving ISD Teachers' Identities." *Dallas Morning News,* February 4. Retrieved January 28, 2011 (http://www.dallasnews.com).

Walters, Glenn. 1990. *The Criminal Lifestyle: Patterns of Serious Criminal Conduct.* Newbury Park, CA: Sage.

Warr, Mark. 2002. *Companions in Crime: The Social Aspects of Criminal Conduct.* New York: Cambridge University Press.

Weaver, Frances M., and John S. Carroll. 1985. "Crime Perceptions in a Natural Setting by Expert and Novice Shoplifters." *Social Psychology Quarterly* 48:349–359.

White, Michael D., and Christopher Fisher. 2008. "Assessing Our Knowledge of Identity Theft: The Challenges to Effective Prevention and Control Efforts." *Criminal Justice Policy Review* 19:3–24.

Weisburd, David, Stanton Wheeler, Elin Waring, and Nancy Bode. 1991. *Crimes of the Middle Classes: White Collar Offenders in the Federal Courts.* New Haven: Yale University Press.

Willison, Robert. 2009. "Applying Situational Crime Prevention to the Information Systems Security Context." In *Perspectives on Identity Theft,* Crime Prevention Studies, vol. 23, edited by M. McNally and G. Newman, 169–192. Monsey, NY: Criminal Justice Press.

Willott, Sara, Christine Griffin, and Mark Torrance. 2001. "Snakes and Ladders: Upper-middle Class Male Offenders Talk about Economic Crime." *Criminology* 39:441–467.

Wright, Bradley R. E., Avshalom Caspi, Terrie E. Moffitt, and Ray Paternoster. 2004. "Does the Perceived Risk of Punishment Deter Criminally Prone Individuals? Rational Choice, Self-Control, and Crime." *Journal of Research in Crime and Delinquency* 41:180–213.

Wright, Richard. 2001. "Searching a Dwelling: Deterrence and the Undeterred Residential Burglar." In *Contemporary Issues in Crime and Criminal Justice: Essays in Honor of Gilbert Geis,* edited by H. Pontell and D. Schicor, 407–418. Upper Saddle River, NJ: Prentice-Hall.

Wright, Richard, and Scott Decker. 1994. *Burglars on the Job.* Boston, MA: Northeastern University Press.

Wright, Richard, and Scott Decker. 1997. *Armed Robbers in Action.* Boston, MA: Northeastern University Press.

INDEX